OTHER VOLUMES IN THIS SERIES

THE
BEST
AMERICAN
POETRY
2011

◊　◊　◊

Kevin Young, Editor

David Lehman, Series Editor

SCRIBNER POETRY
NEW YORK   LONDON   TORONTO   SYDNEY   NEW DELHI

SCRIBNER POETRY
A Division of Simon & Schuster, Inc.
1230 Avenue of the Americas
New York, NY 10020

First Scribner edition September 2011

For information about special discounts for bulk purchases,
please contact Simon & Schuster Special Sales at 1-866-506-1949
or business@simonandschuster.com.

The Simon & Schuster Speakers Bureau can bring authors to your live event.
For more information or to book an event, contact the Simon & Schuster Speakers
Bureau at 1-866-248-3049 or visit our website at www.simonspeakers.com.

Manufactured in the United States of America

1   3   5   7   9   10   8   6   4   2

Library of Congress Control Number: 88644281

ISBN 978-1-4391-8150-8
ISBN 978-1-4391-8149-2 (pbk)
ISBN 978-1-4391-8151-5 (ebook)

CONTENTS

David Lehman was born in New York City in 1948. He was educated at Columbia University, spent two years in England as a Kellett Fellow at Cambridge University, and worked as Lionel Trilling's research assistant upon his return to New York. His books of poetry include *Yeshiva Boys* (2009), *When a Woman Loves a Man* (2005), *The Evening Sun* (2002), *The Daily Mirror* (2000), and *Valentine Place* (1996), all from Scribner. He has edited *The Oxford Book of American Poetry* (Oxford University Press, 2006), *The Best American Erotic Poems: From 1800 to the Present* (Scribner, 2008), *Great American Prose Poems: From Poe to the Present* (Scribner, 2003), among other collections. *A Fine Romance: Jewish Songwriters, American Songs* (Nextbook/Schocken), the most recent of his six nonfiction books, won a 2010 Deems Taylor Award from the American Society of Composers, Authors, and Publishers (ASCAP). An exhibit based on *A Fine Romance* will visit fifty-five libraries in twenty-seven states from May 2011 through April 2012. Lehman initiated *The Best American Poetry* series in 1988. He has received a Guggenheim Fellowship and an award in literature from the American Academy of Arts and Letters. He teaches in the graduate writing program of the New School in New York City.

FOREWORD

by David Lehman

◊ ◊ ◊

What makes a poem great? What standards do we use for judging poetic excellence? To an extent, these are variants on an even more basic question. What is poetry? Poetry is, after all, not a neutral or merely descriptive term but one that implies value. What qualities in a piece of verse (or prose) raise it to the level of poetry? The questions face the editor of any poetry anthology. But only seldom do we discuss the criteria that we implicitly invoke each time we weigh the comparative merits of two or more pieces of writing. And to no one's surprise, it turns out to be far easier to recognize the genuine article than to articulate what makes it so, let alone to universalize from a particular instance. Thus, so astute a reader as Randall Jarrell will linger lovingly on the felicities of Robert Frost's late poem "Directive" only to conclude sheepishly: "The poem is hard to understand, but easy to love."

The standard definitions of poetry spring to mind, each one seeming a near tautology: "the best words in the best order" (Coleridge), "language charged with meaning to the utmost possible degree" (Pound), "memorable speech" (Auden). Other justly celebrated statements may stimulate debate but have a limited practical application. Is poetry the "spontaneous overflow of powerful feelings" (Wordsworth) or is it precisely "not the expression of personality but an escape from personality" (T. S. Eliot)? The statements contradict each other except in the mind of the reader who enjoys with nearly equal gusto the poetry of the Romantic movement, of Wordsworth and Coleridge, on the one hand, and that of the modernists who reacted so strongly against them (Eliot, Pound) on the other.

Poetry is "what gets lost in translation" (Frost); it "strips the veil of familiarity from the world, and lays bare the naked and sleeping beauty" (Shelley); it "is the universal language which the heart holds with nature and itself" (Hazlitt). Although poems do come along that seem to exemplify such statements, the problem remains unsolved except by individual case. Archibald MacLeish's famous formulation ("a poem should not mean / But be") is conceptually useful in a class of writers but leaves us exactly where we started. Asking herself "what is poetry and if you know what poetry is what is prose," Gertrude Stein makes us understand that poetry is a system of grammar and punctuation. "Poetry is doing nothing but using losing refusing and pleasing and betraying and caressing nouns"—a valuable insight, but try applying it to the task of evaluating poems and see if it gets any easier. Wallace Stevens, a master aphorist, has a score of sentences that begin with the words *poetry is*. Poetry is "a search for the inexplicable," "a means of redemption," "a form of melancholia," "a cure of the mind," "a health," "a response to the daily necessity of getting the world right." It is metaphorically "a pheasant disappearing in the brush" and it is also, in one word, "metaphor" itself. The proliferation of possibilities tells us a great deal about Stevens's habits of mind. But epigrams will not help the seasoned reader discriminate among the dozens of poems crying for attention from the pages or websites of well-edited literary magazines.

The emancipation of verse from the rules of yore complicates matters. It is tough on the scorekeeper if, as Frost said, free verse is like playing tennis without a net. (Some varieties of free verse seem to banish ball as well as net.) But even if we set store by things you can measure—rhyme, meter, coherence, clarity, accuracy of perception, the skillful deployment of imaginative tropes—the search for objective criteria is bound to fail. Reading is a frankly subjective experience, with pleasure the immediate objective, and in the end you read and judge the relative value of a work by instinct. That is, you become aware of the valence of your response, whether it is positive or negative, thumbs-up or -down, before you become aware of why you reacted the way you did. There is in fact no substitute for the experience of poetry, though you can educate your sensibility and become better able to summon up the openness to experience that is the critic's first obligation—that, and the ability to pay attention to the poem and to the impact it has made on you. Walter Pater asked these questions upon reading a poem or looking at a picture: "What effect does it really produce on me? Does it give me pleasure? And if so, what sort or degree of pleasure? How is my nature modified by its presence, and under its influence?"

Whatever else it is, American poetry today is as plentiful as it is diverse. And because very good poems may reflect esthetically incompatible ideas, an editor's job has an added complication; one must be willing to suspend one's natural critical resistance. Poetry may happen "in the valley of its saying," in Auden's phrase, but discussions of poetry take place on academic battlefields. There are possibly as many different movements or schools, cliques or cabals, as there are states in the union. Conflicts may erupt, just as states may quarrel over their share of the federal budget. (The budget for poetry is small and exists therefore in an inverse ratio to the intensity of the skirmishing among poets.) The good reader is or tries to be indifferent to all this—to everything, in fact, except his or her own experience, when sitting down with, say, the latest issues of *FIELD, Antioch Review, New England Review,* and *Green Mountains Review.* I can report, having just spent pleasant evenings with these magazines, that there is a wonderful symposium on Richard Wilbur in *FIELD,* that one of Richard Howard's schoolboy memory poems graces *Antioch Review,* that Joanne Dominique Dwyer has a brilliant poem addressed to St. Teresa of Avila in *New England Review,* and that there is compelling work in *Green Mountains Review* from two poets previously unknown to me: Anna Maria Hong and the Canadian poet Robert Bringhurst, whom Stephen Dunn singles out in an interview. Many poems in these and other new journals pass the first and arguably most crucial test a critic asks of them—that they give pleasure, sustain interest, and compel a second reading.

It may be that in specifying these pragmatic criteria, I have strayed from my original question when I meant merely to rephrase it. What do we ask for in poems of high excellence? To answer you need to make a list, and by the time you get to the third or fourth item you realize that no poem can do all the things people expect from poetry, not only because we may be perfectionists when it comes to judging the works of others but because we want mutually exclusive things. Do we read for moral fortitude, humane knowledge that can help us lead our lives? (Thus, to elucidate the dominant strain in Frost's poetry, W. H. Auden quotes Samuel Johnson: "The only end of writing is to enable the readers better to enjoy life or better to endure it.") Or are we more interested in what the scholar calls transcendence and the reader knows to be escape—whether to Xanadu or Byzantium? (Thus Emily Dickinson: "There is no Frigate like a Book / To take us Lands away / Nor any Coursers like a Page / Of prancing poetry.") Perhaps we respond to feats of ingenuity: complicated verse forms mastered and married to colloquial speech, as in Elizabeth Bishop's sestinas: diabolically clever meaning-making puns in the service of a narrative, as in a sonnet sequence by James Merrill. There is a delight in artifice. In past editions, *The Best American Poetry* has published a poem consisting entirely of palindromes (Lydia Tomkiw: "sad as samara, ruff of fur, a ram; as sad as / Warsaw was raw") and another that exemplifies the zeugma in every line (Charles North: "To break the silence or your newly acquired Ming vase, / or raise my expectations and the flag over the Brooklyn Navy Yard"), in addition to tricky sestinas, villanelles, pantoums, centos, traditional sonnets, ballads, the occasional abecedarius, chant royal, and narrative in terza rima, though these are vastly outnumbered by the many varieties of poems in plain speech, such as you will find exemplified by Robert Hass in the 2011 volume ("When the police do a forced entry for the purpose / Of a welfare check and the deceased person is alone, / The body goes to the medical examiner's morgue") and by Mary Ruefle in a completely different way ("I hated childhood / I hate adulthood / And I love being alive").

Marianne Moore valued the "compactness compacted" that she found in Louise Bogan's poems. But excess has its proponents as well, and there will always be those who want the act of writing to be an act of defiance before it is anything else. Too many poems fail because they try too hard to change the world. But then along comes a work proving that poetry does make something happen. The timely cry of protest may have a longer shelf life than poems with immortal designs on them. Consider the case of Allen Ginsberg's "Howl," tried for obscenity in San Francisco in 1957, lionized nationally more than a half century later with the release of Rob Epstein and Jeffrey Friedman's full-length film homage in 2010. The actor James Franco, who has studied creative writing at Columbia, UCLA, and in the Warren Wilson low-residency MFA program, "captures the Ginsberg we hear in our heads and know in our bones," Ken Tucker writes in his review. The acting borders on impersonation. Franco "looks at the camera with Ginsberg's cockeyed, moist deadpan, or reproduces the Elated Allen Grin—an ear-to-ear face-splitter that can vanish in an instant." Ginsberg's "Kaddish" and "America" may be better poems than "Howl," but the latter has become a battle cry for the ages, an American icon as famous as an Andy Warhol soup can.

In sum, we may like poetic conventions and traditions—and we may like seeing them sent up, too. We want poems of eloquence to recite on grave occasions, and at the same time we have a hankering to parody such utterances. We admire the artistry that conceals itself in the finished work. But we are not immune to the charms of the flamboyant or to what Wallace Stevens calls the "essential gaudiness of poetry."

We want something that sounds "at least as alive as the vulgar" (Frank O'Hara) and is in some sense original. All this, and we want the poet to surprise us with lines and phrases that echo in the mind days, even weeks, after we encountered them, because they have insinuated themselves in our consciousness.[1] Everyone has his favorite touchstones. Consider the sequence of ten monosyllables that kicks off Frost's "Directive": "Back out of all this now too much for us." Or the work that the definite article does to separate states of nothingness in the last line of Stevens's "The Snow Man": "Nothing that is not there and the nothing that is." Think of Emily Dickinson's genitive phrases (a "transport / Of cordiality," "the power to die," "A privilege of Hurricane"), of Hart Crane's jolting juxtapositions ("and love / A burnt match skating in a urinal"), or of the amazing things that W. H. Auden can do with even so commonplace a figure as the "journey of life" in his masterly prose poem "Caliban to the Audience."

In his "Essay on Criticism" (1711), Alexander Pope laid down the law for exponents of the heroic couplet. He prized elegance and pith: "True wit is Nature to advantage dressed: / What oft was thought but ne'er so well expressed." For his odes addressing the Grecian urn, the nightingale, and the condition of melancholy, Keats in 1819 went in pursuit of something different: an agency of imagination "capable of making all disagreeables evaporate"—a force of such intensity, and in so close a relationship with Beauty and Truth, that it can redeem "unpleasantness" and bury "repulsiveness." In the American grain, Walt Whitman and Emily Dickinson belong to the Romantic tradition Keats exemplified but·embody two extreme positions. Dickinson says that she knows exactly what poetry is. "If I read a book [and] it makes my whole body so cold no fire can warm me I know *that* is poetry. If I feel physically as if the top of my head were taken off, I know *that* is poetry." Poetry is, then, an intense sensation, not altogether enjoyable, like the "heavenly hurt" in Dickinson's poem that begins "There's a certain Slant of light." Whitman's most memorable criterion is as "hankering, gross, mystical, nude" as the persona of the author of "Song of Myself." Toward the end of his prose preface to the 1855 edition of *Leaves of*

---

1. "It is hard to ask the two questions, 'Is this good, whether I like it or not?' and 'Do I like this?' at the same time: and I often find that the best test is when some phrase, or image, or line out of a new poem, recurs to my mind afterwards unsummoned." T. S. Eliot, "What Is Minor Poetry?" (1944), in *On Poetry and Poets* (New York: Farrar, Straus and Giroux, 1957), p. 50.

Grass, Whitman tells us he makes this demand of a poem, any poem: "Will it help breed one goodshaped and wellhung man, and a woman to be his perfect and independent mate?"

Harold Bloom speaks in awe of the quality of "strangeness" in the canonical works he prizes.[2] I share the conviction that great poems have an uncanny power—uncanny in the loose sense but sometimes also in the Freudian sense that what we repress returns to haunt us. You feel the uncanny at work when you read "Crossing Brooklyn Ferry," and have the illusion, as if by hypnotic suggestion, that Whitman is there in the room with you, his voice in your ear across the divide of a century and a half. The quality of strangeness is perhaps even stronger in "Out of the Cradle Endlessly Rocking," the poem in which Whitman accounts for his calling as a poet. Whitman had been, in Mark Van Doren's character-ization, "a lazy, eccentric, uneducated, unsuccessful, little-known news-paper man" when he underwent the transformation, or endured the vision, out of which all his poetry seems to emanate.[3] But when he sits down to write about the experience that initiated him into manhood and made him a bard, Whitman recalls the moment when, as a boy alone on the shore in Long Island, he heard two mockingbirds sing, and then one stopped singing and the other missed his mate and sang elegiac songs to her, and suddenly Whitman understood his purpose in life, "what I am for." The next words are climactic: "And already a thousand singers, a thousand songs, clearer, louder and more sorrowful than yours, / A thousand warbling echoes have started to life within me, never to die." The eight lines that follow constitute a credo and a vow:

O you singer, solitary, singing by yourself—projecting me;
O solitary me, listening—nevermore shall I cease perpetuating you;
Never more shall I escape, never more the reverberations.
Never more the cries of unsatisfied love be absent from me,
Never again leave me to be the peaceful child I was before what there,
    in the night,

2. " 'Strangeness' for me is *the* canonical quality, the mark of sublime lit-erature. . . . Strangeness is uncanniness: the estrangement of the homelike or commonplace. This strangeness is likely to manifest itself differently in writers and readers. But in both cases strangeness renders the deep relation between sublimity and influence palpable." Harold Bloom, *The Anatomy of Influence: Literature as a Way of Life* (Yale University Press, 2011), p. 19.

3. "Walt Whitman, Stranger," in Mark Van Doren, *The Private Reader* (New York: Henry Holt, 1942), p. 85.

By the sea, under the yellow and sagging moon,
The messenger there arous'd—the fire, the sweet hell within,
The unknown want, the destiny of me.

And here Whitman makes a move that lifts the poem into a higher
realm of strangeness. As if unsatisfied with the epiphany he has
achieved, he renews his quest or request. "O if I am to have so much, let
me have more!" He begs for a "clew," a "word final, superior to all," that
will reveal the full meaning of the parable of the two mockingbirds. And
the sea obligingly "Lisp'd to me the low and delicious word death, / And
again death, death, death, death." The word *death* appears a total of ten
times in the space of five lines, and I submit that the extraordinary force
of the passage owes something to the reader's astonishment at the sight
of Whitman ecstatic with the discovery that death is the "word of the
sweetest song and all songs." This is in another register altogether from
Keats's restrained admission, in "Ode to a Nightingale," that "for many
a time / I have been half in love with easeful Death," but it confirms the
seductive power and uncanny appeal that the death wish has for the poet
in a period of doubt and anxiety. Death is either "the mother of beauty"
(Wallace Stevens) or a carriage driver of marked civility (Emily Dick-
inson), a strangely familiar presence in either case, maternal and kind.

The power of the uncanny is pronounced in Dickinson's "There's
a certain Slant of light." You feel it from the moment you register the
double meaning of "certain" in the first line and the arresting "Heft / Of
Cathedral Tunes" two lines later:

> There's a certain Slant of light,
> Winter Afternoons—
> That oppresses, like the Heft
> Of Cathedral Tunes—
>
> Heavenly Hurt, it gives us—
> We can find no scar,
> But internal difference.
> Where the Meanings, are—
>
> None may teach it—Any—
> 'Tis the Seal Despair—
> An imperial affliction
> Sent us of the Air—

When it comes, the Landscape listens—
Shadows—hold their breath—
When it goes, 'tis like the Distance
On the look of Death—

This cryptic utterance is as much a poem about poetic inspiration as "Out of the Cradle" is. Only in the realm of the uncanny sublime—or in Dickinson's brain, "wider than the sky"—can the trope for illumination, a "Slant of light," so naturally associate itself with "despair." The author, who begins a later poem with the imperative "Tell all the Truth but tell it slant," receives the "certain" gift of heaven on condition that she be wounded in the process. "It is possible to see the greater part of her poetry as an effort to cope with her sense of privation," Richard Wilbur writes, adducing "three major privations: she was deprived of an ortho-dox and steady religious faith; she was deprived of love; she was deprived of literary recognition."[4] For the hurt there is compensation. The "internal" meaning-making power that Wordsworth, a more orthodox Romantic poet, called the "inward eye" enables her to tell "all the Truth" but slant, in riddling poems of extreme brevity. The "very Lunacy of Light," as she calls it in another poem, offers enchantment: bees become butterflies, butterflies turn into swans, and the imagination turns the "meanest Tunes" in the forest into "Titanic Opera." Nevertheless she feels the gift to be oppressive, a burden. In the key phrases, "Heavenly Hurt" and "imperial affliction," the nouns pull in one direction, the adjectives in the other, but that is only right if inspiration is a form of creative despair. The aftereffect of that slant of light, as described in the poem's last stanza, compounds the reader's amazement. "The listening landscape and breath-holding shadows are among Dickinson's finest figurations," in Bloom's words, "but her ellipsis is finer still."[5] The dash that ends the poem, the dashes that punctuate it throughout, proclaim the radical strangeness of her art, a feeling that is strengthened when we encounter a Dickinson poem in which the poet asserts that "success" is understood best by a fallen soldier among the defeated or when we read her pithy definition of "Heaven" as "what I cannot reach!"

Mark Van Doren, whose Columbia University students included Allen Ginsberg and John Berryman, taught that "the one thing which all

4. Richard Wilbur, "Sumptuous Destitution," in Judith Farr, ed., *Emily Dickinson: A Collection of Critical Essays* (Prentice-Hall, 1996), p. 54.
5. Harold Bloom, *The Western Canon* (New York: Harcourt Brace, 1994), p. 303.

new poets possess in common is strangeness." For Van Doren, Robert Frost's strangeness consisted in the "conversational tone" of his blank verse; for Randall Jarrell, the strangeness of Frost's "Directive" is "far under the surface, or else so much on the surface . . . that one slides into it unnoticing." Ever mindful of his surname, Frost sometimes depicts himself as a lonely wanderer on a snowy evening, an alien in the universe. The element of the uncanny is present in such dark, wintry poems as "Desert Places" and "Stopping by Woods on a Snowy Evening." But you find it also in the genial "Mending Wall," one of the poems that prove Frost to be not only subtler than innocents who take him at his word but sophisticates who think they see through the subterfuge. The latter may argue that Frost's poem is an argument against fences, boundaries, and property lines—that he is gently satirizing the laconic neighbor, who quotes the authority of his father: "Good fences make good neighbors." And certainly the poem's speaker does seem to side with the natural forces that want walls to crumble in winter weather. "Something there is that doesn't love a wall," he says to open the poem, and he likes the line enough to repeat it as the poem draws to a close. There is, he points out, no reason for a fence between his property and his neighbor's—no reason beyond the neighbor's seemingly mindless repetition of a father's saying, a local tradition. But you read the poem again slowly and it dawns on you that the facts do not quite line up in support of this reading. You realize that the Frost persona not only joins his neighbor in rebuilding the wall but that it is he who initiates the action; that "mending" in the title is a synonym for healing; and that Frost gives the neighbor the last word. Along the way you come across these lines:

> Before I built a wall I'd ask to know
> What I was walling in or walling out,
> And to whom I was like to give offense.

The pun on *fence* in the last word is an exquisite example of Frost's subtlety. Is a *fence* a means to avoid giving *offense*? Analyzed this way, the poem leads not to an aporia of uncertainty but a surfeit of meaning. "And there," in the words of Wallace Stevens, the poet finds himself "more truly and more strange."

One of the hallmarks of *The Best American Poetry* is that each annual volume in a series now numbering twenty-four reflects the sensibility of a different guest editor, himself or herself a distinguished practitio-

ner of the art. No single volume is definitive; each may be viewed not only as an addition but as a corrective. Kevin Young, who made the selections for *The Best American Poetry 2011,* has established himself as a singularly talented poet and man of letters. *Ardency: A Chronicle of the Amistad Rebels,* his most recent collection, is characteristically larger than the sum of its parts; it is unified in tone, style, subject matter, and ambition. Young comes at you in the form of a minstrel show in one poem, a hymn in another, proverbs and prayers, diary entries and letters, to look at the 1839 slave-ship mutiny with the multiple perspectives the truth calls for. Young has edited several important anthologies. *Giant Steps* in 2000 presented African American poets who had recently come to the fore or were about to do so. Subsequent volumes include anthologies of jazz poems, blues poems, and a selected edition of John Berryman, the white poet who dared to adopt a persona in blackface for his most original work, *The Dream Songs.* Last year brought us *The Art of Losing: Poems of Grief and Healing* (Bloomsbury USA), a collection of poems exemplifying the modern elegy in its various guises and, as Young sees it, six stages of mourning, "from Reckoning to Regret, through Remembrance to Ritual and Recovery" and finally to Redemption. It does not necessarily follow from Mr. Young's previous labors, but there is a strong element of the elegiac in *The Best American Poetry 2011.* There are two poems with "Elegy" in their titles and many more that mourn brother, lover, father, friend. There are poems entitled "Valediction" and "The Funeral Sermon," musings on angels and the afterlife. I hasten to say that there are also poems about banking, coffee, dating, poppies, the disastrous oil spill in the Gulf last year, snow, pears, and the end of a love affair, in forms ranging from an inventory of aphorisms to a crown of sonnets. The alphabetical arrangement of the contents produces serendipitous linkages: the late Rachel Wetzsteon's haiku sequence "Time Pieces" prefigures the haiku stanzas of the poem that follows, Richard Wilbur's "Ecclesiastes II:I."

I favor the idea of being as comprehensive and inclusive as possible when surveying the landscape for an enterprise that confers, in the end, an exclusive distinction. The struggle I have annually is not with unsolvable questions of poetic value, the definition of "America," or the use of a superlative. The struggle I have is simply keeping up with the plethora of poems and poets out there begging for a hearing. Much of the mail I get is gratifying. People write that a volume in the series, or a particular poem, had a decisive effect on them. Contributors say they are happy to be included. They call it an honor. They've been reading

The Best American Poetry and now their own work is in there. Some of the poems we have featured have become poetry standards. It's nice to think that we played a hand in that or in the stubborn refusal of poetry to lose its power of attraction in a period of information overkill.

Poetry is unkillable. The very word is too useful. When he found out that I write poetry, a software manufacturer congratulated me on practicing "a craft that will never become obsolete"—unlike last year's version of this year's operating system. Whether or not he meant to be ironic, the irony is he is right. The desire to write poetry is a precious thing. It turns into a need on the one hand and a habit or practice on the other. If we were making a list of reasons to stay alive, and it seems we keep needing to do so, poetry would occupy a cherished place on the list. We have the testimony of people from any and every class, category, and income bracket. To the extent that we can bring to the publishing of poetry the same imaginative energy that goes into the writing of a poem, we will have succeeded in doing something important for the art itself, for our poets, and for readers prepared to embrace poetry if only it were presented to them in an appealing way.

Kevin Young was born in Lincoln, Nebraska, in 1970. *Most Way Home* (William Morrow, 1995), his first book of poems, was selected for the National Poetry Series and won the Zacharis First Book Award from *Ploughshares*. In 2003 *Jelly Roll: A Blues* appeared from Knopf, was a finalist for both the National Book Award and the *Los Angeles Times* Book Prize, and won the Paterson Poetry Prize. *For the Confederate Dead* won the 2007 Quill Award for poetry and *Dear Darkness* won a 2009 Southern Independent Booksellers Alliance Award in poetry. His most recent book is *Ardency: A Chronicle of the Amistad Rebels* (Knopf, 2011). Young has edited *The Art of Losing: Poems of Grief and Healing,* an anthology of contemporary elegies (Bloomsbury USA, 2010), as well as collections of *Jazz Poems* and *Blues Poems,* a selected edition of John Berryman's poems for the Library of America's American Poets Project, and *Giant Steps: The New Generation of African American Writers* (HarperCollins, 2000). His book *The Grey Album* won the 2010 Graywolf Nonfiction Prize and is forthcoming in spring 2012. A recipient of a Guggenheim Fellowship and the USA James Baldwin Fellowship, he is the Atticus Haygood Professor of Creative Writing and English and curator of literary collections and the Raymond Danowski Poetry Library at Emory University in Atlanta, Georgia.

INTRODUCTION

by Kevin Young

◊ ◊ ◊

POETRY'S NEW ECONOMY

I went into poetry for the money. While mostly a joke, this is the serious kind of joke poetry favors, speaking to some truth beneath the tongue. After all, poetry has afforded me a freedom and sense of form little else could; poetry gives key kinds of strictures, good sense, and the satisfaction of finding your way. I'm not sure why more haven't figured this out—as Robert Graves said, "There's no money in poetry, but then there's no poetry in money, either."

The Great Recession hasn't hit poetry. Rather, poetry, our most lamented yet longest standing of the arts, has hit back—often by taking the recession head-on. In reading hundreds of journals and many online magazines for this year's *Best American Poetry,* I was struck by the number of poems that deal with "Banking" (Cara Benson), class (Erin Belieu's "When at a Certain Party in NYC"), or money's ironic sexiness (Rae Armantrout's "Soft Money"). The poems I encountered take on the world, including the workaday one, with real imagination, giving the lie to the idea that poetry is unconcerned with earthly matters. To me that's exactly where poetry lives—not only in the ether, though it may have its place there, too, but in the dirt and deep mud.

The precision and pleasure of poetry—its economy—has found its way into these pages, often with short lyrics but just as often with the long poem as a way of extending the lyric. The long poems here achieve something that few other art forms can, an intensity and exploration of states neglected by a Twitter feed. Stephen Yenser's meditative "Cycladic Idyll" dares to ponder the pleasures of leisure, or escape, by considering the business of words and their history. He turns his idyll into a consideration of idleness:

To browse idly, to idle on in a brief, worn lexicon, to let it lead me on.

Because I need new old sayings. Because the good ones die too soon.
Because bean by bean fills the bag.

Paul Muldoon's long poem "The Side Project" proceeds with characteristic play and poignancy. The poem is not about a circus but *is* a circus, a three-ring extravaganza filled with spectacle and gab. Muldoon matches the repetition found in a crown of sonnets (and in other of Muldoon's recent poems, such as "The Old Country") with the wild wonder of the sideshow, creating echoes between Jumbo the elephant and General Sherman, whose march appears as a "big caravan / of big cats, top dogs, a performing pig named Lord Byron and, no less proven / in battle, the Missing Link, Frog Boy, / the Human Chimera and the Human Alligator." Pope Pius IX, Brahms, the Bearded Lady, and carpet-baggers all share the big top of Muldoon's imagination to help illuminate the spectacle of nineteenth-century history.

By invoking the sideshow in his title, Muldoon claims poetry as "a side project," strange and wondrous—and in this way central to the culture. I can think of no other art form that would allow and even insist on such connections. Maybe it's life that's a side project to poetry? Poetry where life really lives—not at the edges of culture, but the center ring where song and substance meet, and even parade about.

Our age seems to be an elegiac one. Many of the best poems I came across were elegies—often not just for the dead, as in Erika Meitner's tremendous "Elegy with Construction Sounds, Water, Fish," but for the living, such as Natasha Trethewey's haunting "Elegy." For a while I thought it was just me—after all, having recently edited *The Art of Losing,* a collection of contemporary elegies, I know the elegiac mode can come to be familiar and even comforting. But you can hear the elegiac mood not just in these pages, but on the airwaves and "interweb," too: gone seems to be the bright pop of the years just after the turn of the millennium; after nearly a decade of war in the Middle East, and yet more "limited war" as of this writing, it may be no surprise that even the dance music of our time has a hard-edged sound. Such an edge circles through our best music, which is to say, our lyric poetry.

Even in the long poem the lyric seems to reign. After the narrative 1990s in which "reality" became a story to be scripted on television or otherwise, the current writers of the lyric seem to insist on its flexibil-

ity, on their ability to take from any source to find their own manifold music. This may mean D. A. Powell's "Bugcatching at Twilight"—which ain't about "bugcatching" really—or Maurice Manning's "The Complaint against Roney Laswell's Rooster," which is exactly that. There's a constructed casualness often found in these pages, even in poems one might call neo-formal—though such a term seems useless if it applies only to a school of thought and does not include the "shattered sonnets" of Olena Kalytiak Davis or the stark stammerings of Julianna Baggott's "To My Lover, Concerning the Yird-Swine." That these are all love poems—or at least "lust poems"—indicates the ways in which love creates its own tongue. The archaisms and attitudes of such poems manage to make a music of the past that reflects our refracted times.

Wherever the private has eroded, as in American culture, poets often erect a private language—if only temporarily. This is not a hermetic language, but something less elliptical, closer to the vest, furtive even. It is the furtive tongue that appears, for example, in "August Notebook: A Death" by Robert Hass. The poem begins with a kind of unintelligibility that seems all too fitting in an elegy:

> I woke up thinking abouy my brothr's body.
> That q That was my first bit of early morning typing
> So the first dignity, it turns out, is to get the spelling right.

These typos, these misfires of language, Hass suggests, are forms themselves of mourning. While they must be corrected, the typos tell us something about the initial process of grief. For the grieving, the poem is not just a receptacle for private grief—something that I think marks our elegiac age—nor is it just a place for mourning, but the birthplace of a private language. How do we write a public poem about private pain, our age asks? How do we make the private language of grief intelligible to others?

It seems no accident that Hass turns to the blues to tell some of his brother's story, for the blues use public or shared means—song and rhyme and history—to evoke, and even to mask, a private pain.

> You can fall a long way in sunlight.
> You can fall a long way in the rain.
>
> The ones who didn't take the old white horse
> Took the morning train.

It is history that mourns in Cornelius Eady's "Emmett Till's Glass-Top Casket." Till's mother's bravery in showing the world "what they did to my boy" is the ultimate public mourning; but the exhuming of his remains, and the neglect of his casket, have left the coffin "dry-docked, a tattered mercy hull." The "they" in the poem indicts not just those who committed the original lynching of Till, but a "they" that means us, at least whenever we fail to remember. Eady lets the casket speak: "Once I held a boy who didn't look / like a boy. When they finally remembered, they peeked through my clear top. / Then their wild surprise."

At times the poet wishes to make a monument to the life lost—at others to make something as fleeting as the life's (and death's) "wild surprise." There is the springtime hope of Richard Wilbur's "Ecclesiastes II:I," which uses a spiritual and seasonal history to inspire carrying on, "Betting crust and crumb / That birds will gather, and that / One more spring will come." Wilbur's poem is sure-footed and calming, even in its plangency. Alan Michael Parker's "Family Math" takes up similar matters, seeking the assurance and unchanging figures of mathematics in a world where little works that way, always "More to busy me, more to figure and record. / More to have. More to let go."

But if elegiac, and even apocalyptic, the poems here aren't always reverent about it. Take Farrah Field's sequence of Amy poems, which renders her character's surviving "another apocalypse" with tender humor.

> You were bored when the world ended.
> Popcorn gets stuck in your teeth.
> You'll never have a broken nose.
> Go you on the big boat,
> anti-traveling, dressed too fancy to cross a bridge.

The incongruity of the poem echoes the ironies of the blues. Field's "You're Really Starting to Suck, Amy" also suggests the sonnet form, a poem less of love than of affection for a character whose survival and seeming strangeness is reminiscent of John Berryman's Huffy Henry, updated for a world of "Blogs Galore . . . Fiddle-de-doo. Too much news."

In "Here and There" Billy Collins looks into dark places some may not associate with his work. The common misperception of Collins's work seems confused by his persona of the comedian. But those who

read Collins's work carefully will see that his humor comes from admiration of the world's ironies as well as its pleasures, and often covers a steady skepticism. His poem in *The Best American Poetry 2011* pictures a friend in surgery: "an imaginary surgeon busy / breaking into the vault of her phantom skull." Such imaginaries and interrupting suppositions course through his work, a looking away from the difficult in a furtive effort to praise it. Like Robert Frost before him, Collins's popularity obscures the fearsome heart of his best work. The imaginary surgeon may be a better metaphor than that of the homespun comedian for this kind of poet.

The sonnet, like the McRib, is back. As "little songs," sonnets prove both compact yet ambitious, which may provide a sense of why many writers have turned to them to evoke our moment. The sonnet itself is made up of little moments. In my reading, I found any number of quality poems committed to the form, as in Olena Kalytiak Davis's short sequence, where the sonnet provides an opportunity to shift and even twist syntax, mood matching the form. As their subtitles suggest, Davis's poems are silenced and divided and ultimately moving.

So, too, Patricia Smith's "Motown Crown," a sonnet sequence that evokes the music of the Motor City record label, but also a larger cultural tuning.

> Remembering how love had lied so loud,
> we tangled in the rhythms that we chose.

In contrast, Mary Jo Thompson's "Thirteen Months" revisits "modern love" through a sonnet sequence about an ex-husband once loved, now mourned. What, in the face of death, has love become? Tracing both the seasons and the vacillations of the form itself, the poem shows that poetry can tell a story in a way nothing else can. What the sonnet sequence does—and the other sequences here, such as the late Rachel Wetzsteon's "Time Pieces," do—is to mark the passage of time, its permutations and its recalculations, its winding away through the years, themselves a form of form.

As "pieces of time" these diverse poems, taken from fifty-three different publications, tell us of time's presence, and its possibilities. Memory, once one of poetry's functions through its rhyme and meter, still courses through poems today. In the free verse poem it often occurs as an echo. With the contemporary sonnet, rhymed or not,

memory and time are even more present than in free verse; any sonnet evokes all others.

Poetry may not seek money but it does seek immortality. It does this by evoking forms that are ancient, as in the idyll; by using forms that aren't always conventionally poetic, like the complaint (see Jill McDonough's "Dear Gaybashers"); and by inventing new forms. James Richardson's series of "Ten-Second Essays" covers ground that poems sometimes neglect, elevating the aphorism from wit to witness:

> Sure, no one's listening, English will die in a hundred years, and the far future is stones and rays. But here's the thing, you Others, you Years to Come: you do not exist.

This may be poetry's best trait, a way of saying what the poet saw or dreamt, what she willed into being or what he unwillingly had to get down. "The reader lives faster than life, the writer lives slower," as Richardson writes. If we can have Slow Food, I can't see why we can't have poems, words that slow us down for just a bit, to steady or unsettle us—and the language where we live.

THE
BEST
AMERICAN
POETRY
2011

◊   ◊   ◊

ELIZABETH ALEXANDER

Rally

◊　◊　◊

(Miami, October 2008)

The awesome weight of the world had not yet descended
upon his athlete's shoulders. I saw someone light but not feathered

jog up to the rickety stage like a jock off the court
played my game   did my best

and the silent crowd listened and dreamed.
The children sat high on their parents' shoulders.

Then the crowd made noise that gathered and grew
until it was loud and was loud as the sea.

What it meant or would mean was not yet fixed
nor could be, though human beings ever tilt toward *we*.

from *The American Scholar*

Valediction

◇   ◇   ◇

I know, I know, I know, I know, I know
That I could not have convinced you of this,

But these dark times are just like those dark times.
Yes, my sad acquaintance, each dark time is

Indistinguishable from the other dark times.
Yesterday is as relentless as tomorrow.

There is no relief to be found in this,
But, please, "Yours is not the worst of sorrows."

Chekhov wrote that. He meant it as comfort
And I mean it as comfort, too, but why

Should you believe us? You didn't believe us.
You killed yourself because your last dark time

Was the worst, I guess, of many dark times.
None of my verse could have saved your life.

You were a stranger. You were dark and brief.
And I am humbled by the size of your grief.

from *Cave Wall*

Soft Money

◇   ◇   ◇

They're sexy
because they're needy,
which degrades them.

They're sexy because
they don't need you.

They're sexy because they pretend
not to need you,

but they're lying,
which degrades them.

They're beneath you
and it's hot.

They're across the border,
rhymes with dancer—

they don't need
to understand.

They're content to be
(not *mean*),

which degrades them
and is sweet.

They want to be
the thing-in-itself

and the thing-for-you—

Miss Thing—

but can't.

They want to be you,
but can't,

which is so hot.

from *Poetry*

Postlude and Prequel

◇   ◇   ◇

Would I lie to you? I don't know what to say to you,
and the season is coming into season just now
with long-awaited words from back when we were
friends and still are, of course, but the tides
pursue their course each day. Perturbing elements
listen in the wings, which are coming apart at the seams.
Is it all doggerel and folderol? A cracked knowledge?
Monkey journalism?

This is better than the other overlooked good
that dried up a while back and whispers.
The results, if any, won't last too much longer
and I meanwhile am on my way to correct you
about the tickets and their availability.
We pitch and stiffen, elbowed by traffic mysteriously
descending the other lane of the avenue
as lamps burst in many-benched Central Park.

from *London Review of Books*

To My Lover, Concerning the Yird-Swine

◇   ◇   ◇

Lover,
    Don't let the yird-swine in.
You can feed them at the door.
      Hungry yird-swine.
You can polish their teeth and sharpen their claws,
but never, Lover, never
     let them in.

(Here, I am milksop and blur-blind.
    I'm an ugly welt. I love too much
my own filth.)

Somewhere there are deer
    antler-rushing the hunters.
There are dogs who love chains.
    I love the yird-swine, Lover,
as you do.
    I listen to them tunnel through
the family plots—
they want to eat up from the past
     paw and claw in our bed.

They know that you cannot love me and my
stiff knot buns, worn hornish.
     You hate me
  so well—

so thoroughly
only because you have practiced
(rigorous scales, taskmaster metronome)

hating yourself.

from *AGNI*

When at a Certain Party in NYC

◇   ◇   ◇

Wherever you're from sucks,
and wherever you grew up sucks,
and everyone here lives in a converted
chocolate factory or deconsecrated church
without an ugly lamp or souvenir coffee cup
in sight, but only carefully edited *objets* like
the Lacanian soap dispenser in the kitchen
that looks like an industrial age dildo, and
when you rifle through the bathroom
looking for a spare tampon, you discover
that even their toothpaste is somehow more
desirable than yours. And later you go
with a world famous critic to eat a plate
of sushi prepared by a world famous chef from
Sweden and the roll is conceived to look like
"a strand of pearls around a white throat," and is
so confusingly beautiful that it makes itself
impossible to eat. And your friend back home—
who says the pioneers who first settled
the great asphalt parking lot of our
middle were not in fact heroic, but really
the chubby ones who lacked the imagination
to go all the way to California—it could be that
she's on to something. Because, admit it,
when you look at the people on these streets,
the razor-blade women with their strategic bones

and the men wearing Amish pants with
interesting zippers, it's pretty clear that you
will never cut it anywhere that constitutes
a *where,* that even ordering a pint of tuna salad in
a deli is an illustrative exercise in self-doubt.
So when you see the dogs on the high-rise elevators
practically tweaking, panting all the way down
from the 19th floor to the 1st, dying to get on
with their long-planned business of snuffling
garbage or peeing on something to which all day
they've been looking forward, what you want is
to be on the fastest Conestoga home, where the other
losers live and where the tasteless azaleas are,
as we speak, halfheartedly exploding.

from *32 Poems*

Banking

◇   ◇   ◇

Sometimes I pick up the phone and there is a person
the person speaks.
Sometimes I have spoken first and I say things
like hello is someone there I am here.
I worry sometimes. Sometimes I worry so much
I pick up the phone to call someone to tell them
about my worries. Sometimes they try to talk me out of worrying
but sometimes this doesn't work so I hang up.
When I hang up after efforts to calm me fail I sometimes
call the person back to apologize and worry my apology will not be accepted.
When my apology is accepted I feel better
till I remember the initial worry but only sometimes
my apology is accepted because I have done this before. Maybe more than once.
But when I speak and worry and do not apologize
other people sometimes worry about me.
I speak a lot and apologize less.
On the phone I sound confident sometimes.
I call out of state and leave messages. I do
not leave a return number because I do
not want to speak with the person.
Sometimes the person can get my number anyway because of technology
but they usually do not call back because they are not worried about it.
These people I don't apologize to. Not ever.

from *Boston Review*

JASWINDER BOLINA

Mine Is the First Rodeo, Mine Is the Last Accolade

◇　◇　◇

I'm grateful for the man now nuzzling and elating with my ex-lover.
It's true I loved her, but it's right that someone be with her now
in the dark hour of our republic. Life is no good anymore.
There are no jobs and no money, and it's good
that someone be with her now in street lamps filtering
through sheer curtains at night, the pale approximation of daylight
illuminating the outer slope of my ex-lover's left thigh
and the asymmetrical birthmark located there I thought
resembled the bust of Martin Van Buren
which that man should smooch now and cherish
as I did those tender hours on the other side of time and the republic
when in the opulence of waking I'd move to the window to squint
at the dapper bodies passing which seemed then to know
where they were going in morning. What awaited
when they arrived there. No job, no money,
I'm grateful for the man now nuzzling and elating with my ex-lover,
how she survives with him the dark hour, the sad redundancies,
the human condition so like a phonograph skipping,
which is the condition of urging the same thing over
anticipating a different result. How dull it is,
its mimeographed disasters, dull how the bankers are
offing themselves now in morning again, leaping from windows again,
the republic fretting as if it's the first republic, the first dark hour,

the dull way the man drives daily at daybreak away from my ex-lover
in an extravagant light believing that if he does, that when he does,
he'll be the first to hurt her. O, enduring sun.

from *Black Warrior Review*

The Sink

◊　◊　◊

She loves to talk on the phone
while washing the dinner dishes,
catching up long distance or
dealing with issues closer to home,
the reconnoitring with the long lost
or a recent so-and-so. She finds it
therapeutic, washing down
the aftermath. And that feeling
she gets in her stomach with a loved one's
prolonged silence. And under the sink
in the dark among the L-pipes, the confederate
socket wrenches, lost twine, wire lei,
sink funk, steel-wool lemnisci, leitmotifs
of oily sacraments, a broken compass forever
pointing southeast by east, mold codices,
ring-tailed dust motes from days well served,
a fish-shaped flyswatter with blue horns,
fermented lemures, fiery spectres,
embottled spirit vapors swirling in the crude
next to the Soft Scrub, the vinegared
and leistered sealed in tins, delicious with saltines,
gleaned spikelets, used-up votives. . . .
In the back in the corner forgotten
an old coffee can of bacon fat
from a month of sinful Sundays,
a luna moth embossed, rising—a morning star.

from *The New Yorker*

Off the Nollendorfplatz

◇   ◇   ◇

—*Berlin,* A.D. *2000*

The USSR was splitting at the seams
Before the Wall came down. Two more regimes

And no one will remember what it was,
Except that Baku's oil replaced the Shah's.

My homeland was the stairs and not the steppes:
Odessa. Vodka? Thanks. And with a Schweppes.

It was the Berlin Brits who taught me that.
And I teach them? Back flips. An acrobat,

You might say, since I'm a top. One must give in
Only so far. I'm not a knees-up Finn.

My friends who did go home when all four powers
Pulled out are making book in their off-hours

Or, on the corner selling nested dolls.
I can at least buy better alcohols.

I didn't, you did? Well, free enterprise
Is not just ümlauts on Big Macs and fries.

I'm no dumb muzhik. When I had my pay
I'd go to see—how is it that you say—

The "People's Theatre"—*Volksbühne*. Twice
I saw the Gorkii *Tiefe*. Good advice

On how to be flat broke and how not to be.
It taught me my commodity is me.

In my small way I prosper. I sell sex
And then put on a value-added tax.

Marx himself might admire
Such a laborer worthy of his hire.

from *The Sewanee Review*

Dead Ass

◇ ◇ ◇

In the bodega, a young girl wearing
jeans so tight she has to use turpentine
to get them off, says to her friends,
Damn, it's dead ass raining out!

I was enamored. Instead of cats and dogs,
I pictured donkey corpses falling from
the sky, clogging the gutters.
That's some serious rain.

The song on the radio said that the po-po was:
"tryna to catch me ridin' dirty." I imagined
Chamillionaire wearing a 20-lb. gold chain
with mud dripping off Jesus's shiny toes,
Krazie Bone in four-hundred-dollar jeans,
with grass stains on the knees.

In Oakland, the sound there is "hyphy."
To me, that alien word means gooney-goo-goo.
To me, that word is my dead father's kiss.
But to thousands of youngsters whose trousers sink
below the Plimsoll line of their asses, hyphy
music makes their bodies dip up and down
like an oil drill.

These words make me feel old, and alabaster.
When I hear something new, it's like I discovered it
for the first time, like I excavated it from the mouth

of a teenager. So I dust it off with my fossil brush
and try to jam it into the keyhole of academia.

I am not afraid of dope lyrics, not dope meaning weed
but dope meaning good. My kind uses scrilla to board
up the windows of shook.

Fo'shizzle, crunk, hella: I place in glass jars like rare moths.
I want to hang them on the doors of sonnets
like a welcome sign to an apartment
I don't live in.

from *The New York Quarterly*

Here and There

◇   ◇   ◇

I feel nothing this morning
except the low hum of the ego,
a constant, shameless sound from deep in the rib cage.

I even keep forgetting my friend in surgery
at this very hour.

In other words, a perfect time to write
about clouds rolling in after a week of sun
and a woman beating laundry on a rock
in front of her house overlooking the sea—

all of which I am making up—
the clouds, the house, the woman, even the laundry.

Or take the lights strung in a harbor
that I once saw from the bow of a sailboat,
which seemed unreal at the time and more unreal now.

Even if I were there again at the railing
as I am sitting in a lawn chair today, who would believe it?

Vast maple tree above me, are you really there?
and you, open cellar door,
and you, vast sky with sun and a fading contrail—

no more real than the pretend city
where she lies now under the investigating lights,

an imaginary surgeon busy
breaking into the vault of her phantom skull.

from *Boulevard*

Three Sonnets

◇   ◇   ◇

SONNET (DIVISION)

fuck! i have two loves too, i really do:
my one is blonde, my other's hair is black,
but neither either vice nor virtue lacks
and each complete to me is fair(e) and true.

i have not held them side to side, nor wished
as with less(er) love(s) to have them: back to back.
if evil choose a place to lay its wrack
it lie(s) with "i": that stenched and (w)retched dish

(i has not seen me as they must) of self,
and if me looks i can but lose. suggest me!
take me! then back to unalike give me:
to husband, wife, then back upon my shelf:

here (this) my wicked rest: i scribes this text.
"i" blithely rhymed: fuck! all . . . is aural sex.

Sonnet (motion)

i saw you spin: pause once pause twice pause t(h)rice;
too fast you went for me to catch my love,
from that from then was dizzy as a dove
dipping low as sister hawk after (her) mice.

heads up! head down to draw upon that straw:
i'm sorry love, these teeth were in my mouth
before we met before i knew that south
could be as warm as italy or dawn.

right now, who needs prepare to subjugate?!
i give you my self-portrait: you say: look:
it's fawn meets wolf. it's sex meets book.
it's love, love, it's all, it's not too late:

then push and pull took on "self loved self-hate":
dead on. my god. i won. you fucked me straight.

Sonnet (silenced)

with her unearned admixable beauty
she sat up on the porch and asked for (f)light;
answerable only to poetry—
and love—to make it thru the greyblue night

blew smoke into words and even whiter ghosts
that could see what others in this broad dark
could not: she set to make of nothing most,
better: an everenlightening mark:

ghost gave her this: a piece of flint: that if
you rubbed the right way,
the lightlessness would come down, give up, lift—
and then there would be nothing left to say.

o sterilize the lyricism of
my sentence: make me plain again my love

(my ghost)
(and dumb)

from *Green Mountains Review*

Coffee

◊   ◊   ◊

The only precious thing I own, this little espresso
cup. And in it a dark roast all the way
from Honduras, Guatemala, Ethiopia
where coffee was born in the 9th century
getting goat herders high, spinning like dervishes, the white blooms
cresting out of the evergreen plant, Ethiopia
where I almost lived for a moment but
then the rebels surrounded the Capital
so I stayed home. I stayed home and drank
coffee and listened to the radio
and heard how they were getting along. I would walk
down Everett Street, near the hospital
where my brother was bound
to his white bed like a human mast, where he was
getting his mind right and learning
not to hurt himself. I would walk by and be afraid and smell
the beans being roasted inside the garage
of an old warehouse. It smelled like burnt
toast! It was everywhere in the trees. I couldn't
bear to see him. Sometimes
he would call. He wanted us
to sit across from each other, some coffee between us,
sober. Coffee can taste like grapefruit
or caramel, like tobacco, strawberry,
cinnamon, the oils being pushed
out of the grounds and floating to the top of a French Press,
the expensive kind I get
in the mail, the mailman with a pound of Sumatra
under his arm, ringing my doorbell,

waking me up from a night when all I had was tea
and watched a movie about the Queen of England when Spain was hot
for all her castles and all their ships, carved out
of fine Spanish trees, went up in flames
while back home Spaniards were growing potatoes
and coffee was making its careful way
along a giant whip
from Africa to Europe
where cafes would become famous
and people would eventually sit with their cappuccinos, the baristas
talking about the new war, a cup of sugar
on the table, a curled piece of lemon rind. A beret
on someone's head, a scarf
around their neck. A bomb in a suitcase
left beneath a small table. Right now
I'm sitting near a hospital where psychotropics are being
carried down the hall in a pink cup,
where someone is lying there and he doesn't know who
he is. I'm listening
to the couple next to me
talk about their cars. I have no idea
how I got here. The world stops at the window
while I take my little spoon and slowly swirl the cream around the lip
of the cup. Once, I had a brother
who used to sit and drink his coffee black, smoke
his cigarettes and be quiet for a moment
before his brain turned its armadas against him, wanting to burn down
his cities and villages, before grief
became his capital with its one loyal flag and his face,
perhaps only his beautiful left eye, shimmered on the surface of his Americano
like a dark star.

from *The American Poetry Review*

From the Lives of My Friends

◇   ◇   ◇

What are the birds called
in that neighborhood
The dogs

There were dogs flying
from branch to
branch

My friends and I climbed up the telephone poles to sit on the power lines
        dressed like crows

Their voices sounded like lemons

They were a smooth sheet
They grew

black feathers

Not frightening at all
but beautiful, shiny and
full of promise

What kind of light

is that?

★

The lives of my friends spend all of their time dying and coming back and dying
    and coming back

They take a break in summer
to mow the piss
yellow lawns, blazing
front and
back

There is no break in winter

I fall in love with the sisters of my friends
All that yellow hair!
Their arms
blazing

They lick their fingers
to wipe my face
clean

of everything

And I am glad
I am glad
I am
so glad

*

We will all be shipped away
in an icebox
with the one word   OYSTERS
painted on the outside

Left alone, for once

None of my friends wrote novels or plays, from the lives of my friends came
    their lives

Here's what we did
we played in the yard outside
after dinner

and then
we were shipped away

That was fast—

stuffed
with

lemons

from *The New Yorker*

DENISE DUHAMEL

My Strip Club

◇　◇　◇

In my strip club
the girls crawl on stage
wearing overalls
and turtlenecks
then slowly pull on
gloves, ski masks
and hiking boots.
As the music slows,
they lick the pole
and for a tantalizing second
their tongues stick
because it's so cold.
They zip up parkas
and tie tight bows
under their hoods.
A big spender
can take one of my girls
into a back room
where he can clamp
her snowshoes.

from *DMQ Review*

28

Emmett Till's Glass-Top Casket

◊   ◊   ◊

By the time they cracked me open again, topside, abandoned in a tool-shed, I had become another kind of nest. Not many people connect possums with Chicago,

but this is where the city ends, after all, and I float still, after the footfalls fade and the roots bloom around us. The fact was, everything that worked for my young man

worked for my new tenants. The fact was, he had been gone for years. They lifted him from my embrace, and I was empty, ready. That's how the possums found me, friend,

dry-docked, a tattered mercy hull. Once I held a boy who didn't look like a boy. When they finally remembered, they peeked through my clear top. Then their wild surprise.

from *The New Yorker*

Stays

◊   ◊   ◊

Everything alludes to the mood of us.
This color, for instance, the color of you.
Blood-blue like the walls of the house we share.
Blue-black like the ravels in my hair.

Everything habituates the shatter of our glass.
This tiger of yours that mauls on command.
Or yours, the upper hand of dispute.
The furnace you promised to fix *but good*—

But didn't. But haven't. Or: *Won't. Ain't gonna.*
A tainted summer of untoward words.
The unnerved synapse 'twixt *said* and *heard*.
The lapse in my verve,

The slap of your verbs.
How every well we've dowsed runs dry.
The drowsy *oh wells,* the soused betrothals,
The stab-wounds we dressed up in bedclothes.

Everything augments the flaw of us.
The lusters we lack, the lusts we've glutted,
The delusions we've slutted on analyst's couches.
Your Stalinist urges. My purges. I reach

For the one-two punch of panic pills.
You sit and sort the bills. *A pair of parallel hells.*

The gods that goad us know our names.
The books you read disclaim my pain—

And everything stays the same, the same.

from *Gulf Coast*

ALAN FELDMAN

In November

◊ ◊ ◊

When my daughter calls
and I can hear her baby
crying in the back seat
and she asks, "Dad, would you mind if I stop by
for a quick diaper change and feeding?"—

I'm so glad I picked up the phone,
glad I hadn't set off on my walk,
and quite soon I see her car rolling into the driveway,
and the baby is stretching open her little mouth
and wailing, as babies do—
so enraging not to be able to speak,
not even to be able to think this or that is wrong
except that the whole universe is wrong.

And when they're settled in the little bedroom off the kitchen,
and the baby is sucking noisily,
and then, contented once more,
rolling both eyes, not always in the same direction—
mother and baby in the bedroom
where my daughter herself was once diapered and fed—

I feel so thankful for never having strayed very far
into the wide world, never having served
in the foreign wars of my time, and grief for fathers
who do, the ones swaddled in flags—
maybe because yesterday was Veterans Day,
and though she says she's never done this before,
my daughter tells me she called up a soldier's family she knew

just to say she'd been thinking of them, just hoping
the war we have now will end soon.

And the thin November light is straining through the window curtains
we've never changed,
and I feel thankful for my years right here in this house
the way I imagine a tree might feel thankful
if it were ever given an opportunity to roam around the world—

how it might say, "So good of you, but no thank you,
where would the birds be without me here?—
the ones that fly back unpredictably
and perch in my thinning hair,
this and every November."

from *upstreet*

From "The Amy Poems"

◊   ◊   ◊

AMY SURVIVES ANOTHER APOCALYPSE

You were bored when the world ended.
Popcorn gets stuck in your teeth.
You'll never have a broken nose.
Go you on the big boat,
anti-traveling, dressed too fancy to cross a bridge.
You picked up the phone and put it down,
unsure with where to put your recycling.
You gathered what you meant to sell in a big box,
wondered if you could leave America.
What do you have besides discomfort.
You never bought anyone a present anyway.
The loud smacking has been replaced by
what you think are pigeons but are really nothing.
No one does what you want to do before you.
While talking to yourself, you complained.
You can't think of any jokes
and didn't invent any imaginary friends.
Hang up your hang ups in the empty world.
You finally did the dishes,
the most talented person alive.
What you wear doesn't matter. No one can see you.

Blogs galore. You shaved your legs twice. You shaved
off your mosquito bites. Fiddle-de-doo. Too much news.
This is an on-ramp. You've never flown to Ohio. When a call
came through you hit ignore. It was too cold to talk and carry
pad Thai. Could he find his way around your apartment
in the dark, hold the charcoal behind you, would he know what
he was drawing bent over you on white paper, watching
you wash the window, your back. Fluids on your face.
No one here has visited a functional hospital. The countertop
you were told absorbs citrus not spray ink. You cut a stencil
of a water tower. You were going to be smarter. Connecting
all the freckles on your cousin. Breathing through your nose.
You never know when it's going to snow. Lost across the street
from your house. Mapping stars you can't see. Taking books
around with you. Ho-hum any mess can be cleaned up.

from *LIT*

Morning on the Island

◊   ◊   ◊

The lights across the water are the waking city.
The water shimmers with imaginary fish.
Not far from here lie the bones of conifers
washed from the sea and piled by wind.
Some mornings I walk upon them,
bone to bone, as far as the lighthouse.
A strange beetle has eaten most of the trees.
It may have come here on the ships playing
music in the harbor, or it was always here, a winged
jewel, but in the past was kept still by the cold
of a winter that no longer comes.
There is an owl living in the firs behind us but he is white,
meant to be mistaken for snow burdening a bough.
They say he is the only owl remaining. I hear him at night
listening for the last of the mice and asking *who* of no other owl.

from *The Nation*

Everything Is Nervous

◇   ◇   ◇

How many days I can't think.
So when I do think of blue flowers
it's something to hang on to
something briefly phosphorescent.
To fill the void I watch endless
murders on TV. Potential suspects.
Can the bullets removed from
Vince's body reveal the identity of
the killer? How comforting is this
when I wanted to write a sonnet on mortality?

I remember my mother once planted
lilacs in a hedge. They aren't blue but
that's where my mind goes. The mind
being a nose.

Jojo, we have some questions to ask you,
says the cop.

Blue, the most grateful color.
Who could think of killing
the one they love. He, she. He and
he or she, she, or dog, sky. Suddenly

October cuts the endless summer cold.
But it's still the desert. Hardly green.
It's why I can't think, why the moon is
most at home here. You think it loves

those picturesque fields, those leafy
copses? Hard loves hard.

The air smells like cold iron tonight,
yes it does. It's something to
hang on to. Not like a thought.
Not like heroin in the suspect's pocket.
A secret life weirder than any
Little Rock detectives had ever known.
I bet in Little Rock they have flowers
blue as a blue bucket. Suspects, suspects.
It's not a season if it expects
a conclusion. That's what I think,
because of you.

from *Michigan Quarterly Review*

BENJAMIN S. GROSSBERG

The Space Traveler
Talks Frankly about Desire

◇　◇　◇

Out here the pull of bodies keeps
everything moving. Mass desires
mass, in even the tiniest quantities.
But what differentiates us, this
sentience, is that it isn't simply mass
that compels, but the idea of it:
the weighted notion, the notion
of waiting. A physics of our condition—
you might call it a strange force—
gives the dream of bodies more pull
than those orbiting close. It's as if,
human, your Earth suddenly tore
itself from the Sun, flung itself
chest first into the void, for the idea
of another: a sun whose conversions
were more compelling. You know
all gold's forged in a star's heart?
Well, it's as if your Earth lusted
for a sun that could generate better
luster. No matter the likelihood
of the planet spinning endlessly
forward—bowling ball (blue, marbled)
gliding on a never-ending lane toward
no pins. No matter that the star—
if it existed—might crisp it to coal.
The idea must be satisfied. But

I was going to talk frankly about
desire, wasn't I? Well, I desire
frankly: this dark is cold, and I
distinctly remember back there, still
pulsing, the place where I left my sun.

from *Cave Wall*

Poppies

◇ ◇ ◇

There is a sadness everywhere present
but impossible to point to, a sadness that hides in the world
and lingers. You look for it because it is everywhere.
When you give up, it haunts your dreams
with black pepper and blood and when you wake
you don't know where you are.

But then you see the poppies, a disheveled stand of them.
And the sun shining down like God, loving all of us equally,
mountain and valley, plant, animal, human, and therefore
shouldn't we love all things equally back?
And then you see the clouds.

The poppies are wild, they are only beautiful and tall
so long as you do not cut them,
they are like the feral cat who purrs and rubs against your leg
but will scratch you if you touch back.
Love is letting the world be half-tamed.
That's how the rain comes, softly and attentively, then

with unstoppable force. If you
stare upwards as it falls, you will see
they are falling sparks that light nothing only because
the ground interrupts them. You can hear the way they'd burn,
the smoldering sound they make falling into the grass.

That is a sound for the sadness everywhere present.
The closest you have come to seeing it
is at night, with the window open and the lamp on,

when the moths perch on the white walls,
tiny as a fingernail to large as a Gerbera daisy,
and take turns agitating around the light.

If you grasp one by the wing,
its pill-sized body will convulse
in your closed palm and you can feel the wing beats
like an eyelid's obsessive blinking open to see.
But now it is still light and the blackbirds are singing
as if their voices are the only scissors left in this world.

from *New England Review*

August Notebook: A Death

◇　◇　◇

1. River Bicycle Peony

I woke up thinking abouy my brothr's body.
That q That was my first bit of early morning typing
So the first dignity, it turns out, is to get the spelling right.

I woke up thinking about my brother's body.
Apparently it's at the medical examiner's morgue.
I found myself wondering whether he was naked

Yet and whose job it was to take clothes off
And when they did it. It seemed unnecessary
To undress his body until they performed the exam

And that is going to happen later this morning
And so I found myself hoping that he was dressed
Still, though smell may be an issue, or hygiene.

When the police do a forced entry for the purpose
Of a welfare check and the deceased person is alone,
The body goes to the medical examiner's morgue

In the section for those deaths in which no evidence
Of foul play is involved so the examination
For cause of death is fairly routine. Two policemen,

For some reason I imagine they were young,
Found my brother. His body was in the bed
Which was a mattress on the floor. He was lying

On his back, according to Angela, my brother's friend,
Who lives in the building and is schizophrenic
And always introduced herself as my brother's

Personal assistant, and he seemed peaceful.
There would have been nothing in the room
But the mattress and a microwave, an ashtray,

I suppose, cartons and food wrappers he hadn't
Thrown away and the little plastic prescription
Bottles that he referred to as his scrips.

They must have called the ambulance
And that was probably a team of three.
When I woke, I visualized this narrative

And thought it would be shorter. I thought
That what would represent my feelings
Would be the absence of metaphor.

But then, at the third line, I discovered
The three-line stanza and that it was
Going to be the second dignity. So

I imagine he is in one of those aluminium
Cubicles I've seen in the movies,
Dressed or not. I also imagine that,

If they undressed him, and perhaps washed
His body or gave it an alcohol rub
To disinfect it, that that was the job

Of some emigrant from a hot, poor country.
Anyway, he is dressed in this stanza,
Which mimics the terza rima of Dante's comedy

And is a form that Wallace Stevens liked
To use, and also my dear friend Robert.
And "seemed peaceful" is a kind of metaphor.

2. Sudden and Grateful Memory of Mississippi John Hurt

Because I woke again thinking of my brother's body
And why anyone would care in some future
That poetry addresses how a body is transferred
From the medical examiner's office,
Which is organized by local government
And issues a certificate certifying that the person
In question is in fact dead and names the cause
Or causes, to the mortuary or cremation society,
Most of which are privately owned businesses
And run for profit and until recently tended
To be family businesses with skills and decorums
Passed from father to son, and often quite ethnically
Specific, in a country like ours made from crossers
Of borders, as if, in the intimacy of death,
Some tribal shame or squeamishness or sense
Of decorum asserted itself so that the Irish
Buried the Irish and the Italians the Italians.
In the South in the early years of the last century
It was the one business in which a black person
Could grow wealthy and pass on a trade
And a modicum of independence to his children.
I know this because Earlene wrote a paper about it
In school and interviewed fourth-generation
African American morticians in Oakland
Whose grandfathers and great-grandfathers
Had buried the dead in cotton towns on the Delta
Or along the Brazos River in Texas, passing on
To their children who had gone west an order
Of doing things and symbolic forms of courtesy
For the bereaved and sequences of behavior
At wakes and funerals, so that, for example,
The eldest woman in the maternal line
Entered the chapel first, and what prayers
Were said in what order. During Prohibition
They even sold the white lightning to the men
Who were allowed to slip outside and take a nip
And talk about the dead while the cries
And gospel-song-voiced contralto moans

Of grief that could sound like curious elation
Rose inside. Also the rules for burial or burning.
Griefs and rituals and inside them cosmologies.
And I thought gratefully of Mississippi John Hurt's
Great song about Louis Collins and its terrible
Tenderness which can't be reproduced here
Because so much of it is in the picking
Of the twelve-string guitar and in his sweet,
Reedy old man's voice:

>   When they heard
>   That Louis was dead,
>   All the people dressed in red.
>   The angels laid him away.
>   They laid him six feet under the clay.
>   The angels laid him away.

3.

You can fall a long way in sunlight.
You can fall a long way in the rain.

The ones who didn't take the old white horse
Took the morning train.

When you go down into the city of the dead
With its whitewashed walls and winding alleys
And avenues of autumnal lindens and the heavy bells
Tolling by the sea, crowds
Appear from all directions,
Having left their benches and tiered plazas,
Laying aside their occupations of reverie
And gossip and the memory of breathing—
To hear what scraps you can bring
Of the news of this world where the air
Is thin in the high altitudes and
Of an almost perfect density in the valleys
And shadows on summer afternoons sometimes
Achieve a shade of violet that almost never
Falls across pavements down there. Only the arborist

In the park never comes for new arrivals. He is not incurious
But he loves his work, pruning the trees,
Giving them their graceful life
Toward light, and standing back
To study their shapes, because it is he
Who gets to decide
Which limbs get lopped off
In the kingdom of the dead.

You can fall a long way in sunlight.
You can fall a long way in the rain.

The ones who don't take the old white horse
Take the evening train.

4.

Today his body is consigned to the flames
And I begin to understand why people
Would want to carry a body to the river's edge
And build a platform of wood and burn it
In the wind and scatter the ashes in the river.
As if to say, take him, fire, take him, air,
And, river, take him. Downstream. Downstream.
Watch the ashes disappear in the fast water
or, in a small flaring of anger, turn away, walk back
toward the markets and the hum of life, not quite
saying to yourself *There, the hell with it, it's done.*
I said to him once, when he'd gotten into some scrape
Or other, "You know, you have the impulse control
Of a ferret." And he said, "Yeah? I don't know
What a ferret is, but I get greedy. I don't mean to,
But I get greedy." An old grubber's beard, going gray,
A wheelchair, sweats, a street person's baseball cap.
"I've been thinking about Billie Holiday, you know
if she were around now, she'd be nothing. You know
what I mean? Hip-hop? Never. She had to be born
at a time when they were writing the kind of songs
and people were listening to the kind of songs

she was great at singing." And I would say,
"You just got evicted from your apartment,
you can't walk, and you have no money, so
I don't want to talk to you about Billie Holiday
Right now, OK." And he would say, "You know,
I'm like Mom. I mean, she really had a genius
For denial, don't you think? And the thing is,
You know, she was a pretty happy person."
And I would say, "She was not a happy person.
She was panicky and crippled by guilt at her drinking,
Hollowed out by it, honeycombed with it,
And she was evasive to herself about herself,
And so she couldn't actually connect with anybody,
And her only defense was to be chronically cheerful."
And he would say, "Worse things than cheerful."
Well, I am through with those arguments,
Except in my head, though I seem not to be through with the habit—
I thought this poem would end *downstream downstream*—
of worrying about where you are and how you're doing.

from *The Paris Review*

Lighthead's Guide to the Galaxy

◇　◇　◇

Ladies and gentlemen, ghosts and children of the state,
I am here because I could never get the hang of Time.
This hour, for example, would be like all the others,
were it not for the rain falling through the roof.
I'd better not be too explicit. My night is careless
with itself, troublesome as a woman wearing no bra
in winter. I believe everything is a metaphor for sex.
Love-making mimics the act of departure, moonlight
drips from the leaves. You can spend your whole life
doing no more than preparing for life and thinking
"Is this all there is?" Thus, I am here where poets come
to drink a dark strong poison with tiny shards of ice,
something to loosen my primate tongue and its syllables
of debris. I know all words come from preexisting words
and divide until our pronouncements develop selves.
The small dog barking at the darkness has something to say
about the way we live. I'd rather have what my daddy calls
"skrimp." He says "discrete" and means the street
just out of sight. Not what you see, but what you perceive,
that's poetry. Not the noise, but its rhythm; an arrangement
of derangements; I'll eat you to live: that's poetry.
I wish I glowed like a brown-skinned pregnant woman.
I wish I could weep the way my teacher did as he read us
Molly Bloom's soliloquy of yes. When I kiss my wife,
sometimes I taste her caution. But let's not talk about that.
Maybe Art's only purpose is to preserve the Self.

Sometimes I play a game in which my primitive craft fires
upon an alien ship whose intention is the destruction
of the earth. Other times I fall in love with a word
like "somberness." Or moonlight juicing naked branches.
All species have a notion of emptiness, and yet
the flowers don't quit opening. I am carrying the whimper
you can hear when the mouth is collapsed, the wisdom
of monkeys. Ask a glass of water why it pities
the rain. Ask the lunatic yard dog why it tolerates the leash.
Brothers and Sisters, when you spend your nights
out on a limb, there's a chance you'll fall in your sleep.

from *jubilat*

K . A . H A Y S

Just As, After a Point, Job Cried Out

◊   ◊   ◊

The soil froze, cursing the weather. It turned a stoic face
to winter's switchblade and brass knuckles

so that when the warm rain came, the soil said, Go on,
there's no room for you now. Let the backyards

pool up, and the river pitch to the bridges, dragging
the bridges down. Now the billboards will become great

silent rafts so anyone can climb on them and look out,
saying, I would have done the same.

When the water covered the tree trunks and crept up,
the ground shrugged. See, it said. Now,

weather, do you understand? Soon,
there will be no resting place.

from *Black Warrior Review*

Having Intended to Merely Pick on an Oil Company, the Poem Goes Awry

◊ ◊ ◊

Never before have I so resembled British Petroleum.
They—it?—are concerned about the environment.
I—it?—am concerned about the environment.
They—him?—convey their concern through commercials,
in which a man talks softly about the importance
of the Earth. I—doodad?—convey my concern
through poems, in which my fingers type softly
about the importance of the Earth. They—oligarchs?—
have painted their slogans green. I—ineffectual
left-leaning emotional black hole of a self-semaphore?—
recycle. Isn't a corporation technically a person
and responsible? Aren't I technically a person
and responsible? In a legal sense, in a regal sense,
if romanticism holds sway? To give you a feel
for how soft his voice is, imagine a kitty
that eats only felt wearing a sable coat on a bed
of dandelion fluff under sheets of the foreskins
of seraphim, that's how soothingly they want to drill
in Alaska, in your head, just in case. And let's be honest,
we mostly want them to, we mostly want to get to the bank
by two so we can get out of town by three and beat
the traffic, traffic is murder, this time of year.
How far would you walk for bread? For the flour
to make bread? A yard, a mile, a year, a life?

Now you ask me, when are you going to fix your bike
and ride it to work? Past the plain horses
and spotted cows and the spotted horses and plain cows,
along the river, to the left of the fallen-down barn
and the right of the falling-down barn, up the hill,
through the Pentecostal bend and past the Methodist
edifice, through the speed trap, beside the art gallery
and cigar shop, past the tattoo parlor and the bar
and the other bar and the other other bar and the other
other other bar and the bar that closed, where I swear,
Al-Anon meets, since I'm wondering, what is the value
of the wick or wire of soul, be it emotional
or notional, now that oceans are wheezing to a stop?

from *New Ohio Review*

JANE HIRSHFIELD

The Cloudy Vase

◊   ◊   ◊

Past time, I threw the flowers out,
washed out the cloudy vase.
How easily the old clearness
leapt, like a practiced tiger, back inside it.

from *McSweeney's*

God's Promises

◇   ◇   ◇

I, the Lord, will make barren
your fields and your fairways.
Your refrigerators will be empty,
no steaks and no leg bones,
no butter and no cornbread.
And I will remove your screen doors,
force the mosquitoes indoors
where you lie on the bed undead.
For my house you have not readied,
no flat screen and no broadband.
My habitation is a wasteland
of furniture from motel rooms.
I will send the ostrich and badger
in herds through your wrecked rooms;
your beds will be entered by turnstile;
the floor will seethe with bees.
For my house is but a prefab;
its roof lets in my rain.
Woe is the Lord of Heaven
who has no mansion on earth.
Cries are heard from my fish traps,
crows flap on my hat rack,
pandemonium at the threshold
as the owls and bats flit in.
Silence reigns in the last place
and the first place has no sway.
For my knife-edge is impatient,
my ledge crumbles like cake.
I have warned you to beware.

You await a handsome savior,
but the plain man draws near . . .

(Zephaniah)

from *Poetry*

The Funeral Sermon

◇ ◇ ◇

Almost droll
in its assault on *magisterial,*
my father's funeral
sermon made me prowl,
—agitated—from bean casserole
to escarole
salad, then taco casserole,
and back all afternoon, in thrall
to Dad's every growl,
cramped certitude, and corporal
wavering lost to shrill
sacral
cant: The pastoral
story was Dad's own, though, frail
as it is: faith and God steamroll
death. His wife's and daughter's role
was to die—a trial
of faith, not cruel
so much as natural,
when the supernatural
is, as it was for him, literal.
His cloistral
withdrawal, according to the minister's drawl,
was grace, and his temporal
forfeitures fat collateral
on eternity. It felt surreal
(can there be a funeral
without, now, the word *surreal*?)
to hear Dad's stoic control

and loneliness spiral
heavenward on genial praise, real
enough for the general,
one supposes. An orchestral
hymn flared through the stereo's cloth grill.
Cold waves over the deep water roll,
we sang, some voices shrill,
mine guttural,
my brother's slow as a crawl—
our voices one and several,
a visceral,
not unmagisterial,
chorale.

from *Poetry*

From Holding Company

◊   ◊   ◊

BEREFT

Seemingly without consequence, we're all here,
a tribunal of insomniacs. I'm the one leaping,
a dolphin catching treats. The room smells
of sand-crusted seaweed. In a single evening, soft women
have moved like wind-blown clouds over my dark body.
Your wife is not at home but hosting this spell
of fine light slanting through poplars outside
a bedroom window. Language died the moment
desire disrobed and bodies made fine striations
of solar flares. And while you sleep, a mouse
sniffs its snout along a baseboard floor.

LYING

Such a dislike for transparence, he'd overdid
himself, monitoring caves. True enough,
he wanted a row of filaments inside like Times Square.
The sockets were dead. To live freely
presages danger in a democracy: major irony.
Such a gift he possessed of reading facial bones,
even in the dark. Hearts placed in a dream
over his city, each encounter an exercise in touch ups.
In every house, portraits abound. Last night,
he fell asleep listening to sad people sing.

THE GIANT SWING ENDING IN A SPLIT

Why was I ashamed to be seen on the waterfront
with her? We both felt the past slip
from our shoulders, rose-lipped and listening to
jet engines Doppler across the night.
Wasn't I also me when I lay with her?
Maybe frighteningly more. My sleepsmile
and low whispers hers, too. O,
delicious agony, I'm divided right
to my body's historic wharf. I only trust the sweat
salting down my back her fingernail tracks.

NARCISSUS

Some years ago I recall someone paid attention,
like when an invalid half rises, gripping an armchair—
the street captains and priests busy clicking latches.
The homeless withdrew their luxuries. At night,
distant highways whispered long sighs to the world.

How many hours have I spent crushing mangrove leaves,
turning my face to the unbearable grandeur of this heat-soaked
sky? When I spun around, I felt suddenly filled with birds.
Still, I returned, wallowing in the brothels of myself.
I thought of my life, caressing more ruins.

from *At Length*

Notebooks

◇　◇　◇

What good are notebooks?
—Talking Heads, "Life During Wartime"

I crave them as if craving something carnal,
blankness of pages erotic, clean with sensual
possibilities and ready to be dampened
by my insistent ink, swirls of language

made plain on thin blue lines taut
as tightrope. I collect them like other women
collect shoes or boyfriends, fingering pristine
pages while standing hushed in aisles

of bookstores and stationery shops,
stroking plush-covered ones with a single
finger, loving floral-print ones more
than actual flowers, needing another and

another until my house is overrun
with them, and they start arranging
cocktail hours and support groups—
for the ones I have not written in

grow lonely, and the ones managing
the burden of my desperate handwriting
need someone to talk to, peers to confide in
about these dog-eared secrets and semi-scribbled

imaginings, covert half-truths, outright lies.
How they congregate around my bed,
waiting for me to pick one up, start
another hazy page of scrawls and arrows,

cross-outs and restarts, confessions
that will never be confessions until
I judge them fit for judgment. Sometimes
when fate has flattened me with its one

hard fist, only the black-and-white
composition notebooks of childhood
will do, marbled covers unchanged
from when I first learned cursive—

one letter reaching for the next
in the crazy tilting of my untested hand.
Only those wide-ruled lines will do,
those patient beginnings.

from *River Styx*

Andrew Wyeth, Painter, Dies at 91

◊ ◊ ◊

A weathered barn on a hilltop; a nude woman
sprawled on the slope
below.

A giant squid rises out of a hayfield, & the barn
is compassed in tentacles
then a cloud of ink.

A man with a fountain pen in his hand
& a pitchfork
in his back

walks the cow-path around the barn
& tells the beauty
on the hill

to step to it. It's as if her freckled skin
is newly charcoaled
& the hayloft

a smokescreen. The cows can't be heard for certain
within the ink blot,
but deer

creep to the edge of the field on
delicate feet.

from *The Believer*

JENNIFER KNOX

Kiri Te Kanawa Singing "O Mio Babbino Caro"

◊   ◊   ◊

When I was a younger thing, a voice unscarred
by scratches, growl or clashy wobble rung
cheesy in my ears—dippy—insincere. I'd go
off long and loud in dingy bars on Emmylou—
those 99.9% pure pipes moved my snide heart
less than Debbie Boone. Angels were for Oprah—
give me wolves. Give me Callas—her final flailing
swipe at the rope—a yelp—before she tumbles
off the cliff. Give me Caballé, the wrecking ball—
her vengeance call, a roaring firehose of fat.

But this: only wide open *ah* and *oh*—bright as
knives but weightless as prism-pitched rainbows—
clear Karo syrup, charmed (I'm sure), snaking
its way into cloudless blue sky—a cotton Cadillac
taking the curve magnet tight—no gap—cresting
the hill and not falling back to earth but flying off—
but no rollercoaster dip in the stomach—only more
air and *ooo*. Glitchless. *What's happening*
to me? I ask my parrot who has been lulled
to sleep by her sweatless, even song.

from *LIT*

YUSEF KOMUNYAKAA

A Voice on
an Answering Machine

◊ ◊ ◊

I can't erase her voice. If I opened the door to the cage & tossed the
magpie into the air, a part of me would fly away, leaving only the
memory of a plucked string trembling in the night. The voice unwinds
breath, soldered wires, chance, loss, & digitalized impulse. She's telling
me how light pushed darkness till her father stood at the bedroom door
dressed in a white tunic. Sometimes we all wish we could put words
back into our mouths.

I have a plant of hers that has died many times, only to be revived
with less water & more light, always reminding me of the voice caught
inside the little black machine. She lives between the Vale of Kashmir
& nirvana, beneath a bipolar sky. The voice speaks of an atlas & a mask,
a map of Punjab, an ugly scar from college days on her abdomen, the
unsaid credo, but I still can't make the voice say, Look, I'm sorry. I've
been dead for a long time.

from *The American Poetry Review*

Snow

◊   ◊   ◊

Snow that covers us from above,
Cover us more deeply.
Whiten the city with its houses and churches,
The red house and the yellow house,
The port with its ships.

Cover the Garden House
Where we could never get warm.
There was a fireplace so we learned to build fires.
We had a baby so we walked in the rain.

Cover the fields, cover the trees,
The river beneath us prodding its black stones,
The suffering of which I wasn't aware.

Cover the house where I grew up in New Jersey,
The basement where I learned how to paint,
To hammer a nail, to cut a silk screen.

The harpsichord I built,
The piano I played,
The attic where I stood alone in the cold
Listening for something, I didn't know what.

I hid a book in the eaves,
I couldn't find it when we moved.

Snow that covers us from above,
Cover us more deeply.
Cover the rooftops,
Cover the sea.

from *Salmagundi*

The Pilgrim Is Bridled and Bespectacled

◇　◇　◇

World, I honor you.
After everything
we've been through

I honor you and take you with me
up the mountainside
where we will live
in wonderment.

I take you to the desert
where we shrivel like worms
and become tongues
for other people to kiss with.

World, there are two baskets
on my back.
Fill them. Fill them with fruit
and more fruit.

Or fill them with whatever
is customary
but tell me it is fruit.
Call it something good.

World, some have satisfied their thirst.
But I am the crying-out animal
who can see in the dark.
Forgive me.

from *Ploughshares*

The Complaint against Roney Laswell's Rooster

◊ ◊ ◊

Attention, Mister Roney Laswell—Roney,
short for Tyrone, I hear—
the hour your rooster blows,

four, is two too early.
Another two would do. Go,
speak to your rooster, Roney.

from *New South*

Pears

◊　◊　◊

The pears are all buttocks and hips. They lie on their sides, asleep in the blue bowl. Mothers at rest in a swimming pool of the gods, surrounded by sky.

The heads are so small, without features. They could be anyone and therefore are no one, their slumber as anonymous as their faces.

Like those clay statuettes thousands of years old: the breasts, the wide hips, the tiny faces as blank as thumbs, the legs crumbled to sand eons ago.

The bright plaza painted blue in the sunlight. The one by the ruins of the Aztec temple. Did mothers once sleep behind shutters in the afternoon, dreaming of husbands and lovers who dreamt of them, dreaming of children who woke beyond their dreams as husbands and daughters?

The slope of my wife's hip as she sleeps, turned away from me. How many times have I reached for her and my hand come away with the after-birth of a dream that vanished like phosphorescent foam?

The woman washed up on shore. No one could identify her. As her body lolled back and forth in the tide, no one could tell if she was arriving or departing.

from *Sentence*

Dear Gaybashers

◊　◊　◊

The night we got bashed we told Rusty how
they drove up, yelled QUEER, threw a hot dog, sped off.

Rusty: *Now, is that gaybashing? Or
are they just calling you queer?* Good point.

Josey pitied the fools: who buys a perfectly good pack of wieners
and drives around San Francisco chucking them at gays?

And who speeds off? Missing the point, the pleasure of the bash?
Dear bashers, you should have seen the hot dog hit my neck,

the scarf Josey sewed from antique silk kimonos: so gay. You
missed laughing at us, us confused, your raw hot dog on the ground.

Josey and Rusty and Bob make fun of the gaybashers, and I
wash my scarf in the sink. I use Woolite. We worry

about insurance, interest rates. Not hot dogs thrown from F-150s,
homophobic freaks. After the bashing, we used the ATM

in the sex shop next to Annie's Social Club, smiled at the kind
owner, his handlebar mustache. Astrud Gilberto sang *tall and tan*

and young and lovely, the girl from Ipanema . . . and the dildos
gleamed from the walls, a hundred cheerful colors. In San Francisco

it rains hot dogs, pity-the-fool. Ass-sized penguins, cock after cock in azure acrylic, butterscotch glass, anyone's flesh-tone, chrome.

from *DMQ Review*

Elegy with Construction Sounds, Water, Fish

◇   ◇   ◇

A nail gun fires into wooden scaffolding up the hill—
the skeleton of a roof unfolding above the trees.
Rat tat tat. Bunk bunk bunk. There is music,
and there is music—the tap of a hammer
smoothing out a mistake. Tall hillside grass
sways, and the houses tucked into the valley
don't do anything. They don't rock
like the black shoulders of mourners.

Something is chirping in the yard,
but in Yiddish the skies are empty
of birds. An air-conditioning unit hums.
The mountains cup the houses the way
a boy might half-moon his hands together
to catch water from a hose that arcs
and splats on cement—skin of water, skin
of pavement. We spend all night outside

staining the deck. The night my grandmother dies
we have to do something. The night my grandmother dies
I dream of my dead friend Chris. He gives me
a fish and I skin it, roll up its white flesh,
secure it with a toothpick on a basement work table.
There is a dearth of fish in Yiddish. In my dream,
Chris and I go out at sunset, roam the streets
of what seems like Queens. He walks off

with his school bag slung sideways across his chest
before I can show him the Friday ladies in hats,
the Friday candy store, the whiskered carp slapping
the sides of white bathtubs of my childhood
while my grandmother, bare-armed, wigless,
stands over the kitchen sink with a mallet.
Whatever is chirping in the tall hill grass
won't quit. Yiddish is a world devoid

of trees. My grandmother is dead.
We each took turns burying her
with the rounded side of a shovel,
the sluice of earth sliding over metal.
The dirt hit her wooden box—each clod
and rock. You've heard the sound before.
There is clover in the yard, but Yiddish
has almost no flowers. My aunt will set

a white towel, a pitcher of water
on the stoop. We will wash death
from our hands before we enter her house.
There is music, and there is music.
There is water from a plastic pitcher
hitting slate pavers, silenced by skin.
There are valleys with houses tucked
into them and something trilling

in the grass, and there is Yiddish—
my grandmother's Galicianer accent,
shorthand for a thumping resilient
nameless thing that refuses to leave us,
refuses to sing.

from *The Virginia Quarterly Review*

The Side Project

◊   ◊   ◊

I

Forty years of Jumbo doing a one-handed handstand while some geek
simultaneously bites the head off a Wyandotte cock
and the band plays a Hungarian Dance by Brahms
doesn't mean we're all on the same page. No Human Skeleton or Bearded
        Lady will primp
less for a small show than a great. A unicorn may graze
the dunes in all their vagaries
and never quite grasp the point
its horn is secured by Bondo.
Though a Norwegian bareback artiste may extend her liking for mere glogg
to mulled wines in general, a curl of the upper lip is a sign of colic
fairly specific to horses. Our impulse to give anything a try
takes in both sudatory
and Psalter, don't you know? I know from your well-documented propensity
        to moan
that your page would be very far from mine
even in the first of those *Syllabi*
Errorum Pope Pius IX, poor slob,
one-handedly set down in 1864, the very year Forepaugh first put a unicorn in
        clover
and Sherman's march to the sea meant the Civil War was pretty much over.

II

Forty years since we set up winter quarters in Florida and the hay-bale
first tumbled into the economy of scale,

what with the cost
per unit going down as surely as an elephant will be gussied
up for the "come in." Arachne swallowing a sword all the way to the hilt
as the crowd inches into the tent. The frost now having taken such a hold
the citrus crop is under threat. Each orange and lemon moving in its own
        sphere.
As for the ignominies suffered by Lucifer,
a four-horned goat
who found himself frozen out by the big cat
contingent from their big car, they stab me in the heart.
Who hasn't woken up screaming in a four-poster elephant herd?
When we fell in love, the consequences for the Human Skeleton
and the Bearded Lady who operates a printers' guillotine
were simply dire.
Now Arachne is wearing what looks like ecclesiastical attire.
She hauls herself up through the rigging while the big cats adjourn
to their big caravan to ponder the laws of exponential decay and exponential
        return.

III

Forty years ago we realized that our impulse to be open
to pretty much anything may not run to the Feejee Mermaid (half-guppy, half-
        gibbon)
any more than a dead saint who may still sweat
the Precious Blood so beloved of Pius IX, poor sod.
I imagine Barnum taking umbrage
at the suggestion he'd staged Sherman's march
as a diversionary tactic. The unicorn Forepaugh turned out has the clover-
        slobbers.
The umbrella-mouth gulper
is an eel that can take in damn nearly an entire clover-field
but, like yourself, probably doesn't perform fellatio
and probably isn't impressed by an unbitten
Wyandotte's felt head with its eye still bright as a button
the geek holds up to the incoming crowd. That same Hungarian Dance music
by Brahms. It's pretty clear Sherman was heading for Moscow
the way he eased his way with pig-grease
even before the carpet-baggers

would reveal themselves most by what they most revile.
At least everyone in a circus crowd accepts he's no more than part of the rank
        and file.

IV

Forty years from the first time we heard the strains of that Hungarian
Dance by Brahms and did our best not to picture Jumbo hit by an unscheduled
        freight train
in a marshalling yard in Ontario, Arachne was making straight the path
over a mud-bath
while Sherman gathered his unruly
troops with a drum-roll
usually associated with a firing squad. You and I had hardly gone beyond our
        first peck
at a Coney Island frankfurter stand when I spotted the Norwegian bareback
artiste with one foot on the unicorn-sire
and one on Barnum, as we'd come to know the chief impresario.
While the spotlight would ballyhoo
in a figure-8 over an elephant folio
poster announcing General Tom Thumb and Jenny Lind, the Swedish
        nightingale,
the Bearded Lady never lost her cool.
Arachne's insistence that an aerialist is not an acrobat
but a fallen angel serves only to perpetuate
your idea that manna from heaven
may be found to an unprecedented degree in Gray's Papaya at Eighth Avenue
        and West 37.

V

Forty years to the day when a trawl through Jumbo's stomach would have
        brought up keys,
nuts, screws, washers, bolts, brass tacks, geegaws,
a bag of coins with which Judas Iscariot
had been bought off for his part in the Papal masquerade
by that poor sod Barnum, or Dan Rice,

complete with performing pig. You and I know what it is to have a protective
     layer of ice
to stave off that greater freeze, know that it's not an out-and-out hoax
when the Bearded Lady enters the blade-box
to be sawn in half. That may not be a spurt
of blood as such but we know this is no less a blood-sport
than when Arachne ran into a little impediment as the crowd inched into the
     tent.
Our impulse to apply yellow Centaur liniment
to Jumbo or his cousin, Toung
Taloung, was ill-founded, a wrinkling of the nose coupled with a looseness of
     the dung
being a sign of croup in the mahout. It was strictly of her own accord
the Bearded Lady was cut into quarto
and bound in stillborn calf-hide
like your run-of-the-mill Feegee Mermaid or Pickled Punk malformed in his
     formaldehyde.

VI

Forty years of Barnum trying to establish the cost per unit of promoting
     Commodore Nutt
as the new Tom Thumb, of Arachne's working without a safety net
at any moment likely to foreground the rot
in erotica. What must have made Arachne finally see red
was the realization that, at the 1846 Papal Conclave,
Pius IX had overseen the Bearded Lady being sawn in half
by the moderate and conservative factions. For it would surely not be lost
on Pius IX that an aerialist
is no mere acrobat, given his powers
of infallibility, don't you know? Forty years of Jumbo showing his prowess
in the one-handed handstand
while some geek simultaneously decapitates a rooster. The tune that will come
     to haunt
me as Lucifer leads the "come in" and the geek spits the head into the front
     stalls
will rise above the big cat calls.
It's that same old Hungarian Dance tune

played on a cornet from a unicorn that once grazed the dunes
in all their vagaries. We took it as a signal for Frog Boy and the Human Chimera
     to wreak
vengeance on Barnum for being such an out-and-out control-freak.

VII

Forty years to the day since Sherman set off from Atlanta for Savannah with his
     big caravan
of big cats, top dogs, a performing pig named Lord Byron and, no less proven
in battle, the Missing Link, Frog Boy,
the Human Chimera and the Human Alligator. Barnum still insisting this isn't
     a decoy
to distract us from some main event. Your insisting, meanwhile, this was chalk
from Arachne's hands on my pants. Some days it looked as if Lucifer might stalk
a raggedy-ass lion
to pull down the news from behind the headline.
It was 1867 when the frankfurter trend
took off on Coney Island and it must indeed have marked the end
of an era to a goat with four horns,
never mind the first unicorn
Forepaugh had turned out under the unicorn nomenclature.
The Missing Link and the Human Alligator
now found themselves going off behind the generator truck
to work up their new trick
while I found myself checking for symptoms of croup
in both the Norwegian bareback artiste and Arachne, then the new girl in the
     trapeze-troupe.

VIII

Forty years of Forepaugh or Dan Rice or Barnum IX heaping ignominy upon
     ignominy
really doesn't mean
we're all of a like mind as to how to deal with the rash
of pickpockets at a matinee, never mind the crash
in the marshalling yard in Ontario that thrust my little side project front and
     center.

Jumbo would no more truly benefit from Centaur
Liniment than, in the Civil War, Barnum truly brought cheer
to the country with a Pickled Punk in a Mason jar.
It was in Ontario the Norwegian bareback artiste's triumphing over Arachne
as she might over an unbroken
Appaloosa came to a sudden halt. Now the Missing Link prevailed over *Dictatus*
    Papae
in the way Gray's Papaya
has prevailed over Papaya King.
I know your propensity for believing Barnum was no more subsumed by
    Ringling
than Lee was routed by Sherman's Savannah campaign
but you've got to admit the "come in"
is an effective way of consigning a crowd to the peripheries.
It was in Ontario you and I would first find a way of staving off that even
    greater freeze.

IX

Forty years after I stumbled upon the Norwegian bareback artiste, herself
    without a stitch,
helping Barnum to make a pitch
for the upcoming gigs at Gethsemane and Golgotha, I found Arachne forcing
    mere
glogg down the Good Thief's throat. Forepaugh, meanwhile, in an unpub-
    lished memoir,
would admit to having hired the gang of pickpockets
that fleeced the matinee crowd. I imagine you as a mahout lying under a spigot
in Coney Island and wrinkling your nose
as you pull down the news
behind the headline that you've finally had your first peck of a frankfurter.
Forty years since we set up winter quarters
in Florida and the Bearded Lady was cut into duodecimo,
not even the elephant folio could subsume
Tom Thumb and Jenny Lind the way Sherman took in Atlanta.
What you found on my pants on Coney Island
wasn't chalk but rosin, don't you know? I suppose that, prior to the St. Louis
    hippodrome,
the hope had been that Arachne's spiking her red wine with equal parts rum

and potato akvavit
might allow her to bounce off the Appaloosa's rosin-dappled safety net and
     land on her feet.

X

Forty years since Sherman was attacked by Confederate guerillas from the rear
and you and I first settled into our starring roles in our own little raree
show cum snake-oil
circus it's pretty clear we've found a way to foil
most guerilla attacks by making a pre-emptive strike on the "citrus crop."
I'm no more interested in an Arachne showing me the ropes
than in a Norwegian bareback artiste and her umbrella-mouth gulper eel.
I imagine a Norwegian bareback artiste, as recently as 1864, setting the Papal seal
on a Mason jar in which is suspended the first (and last) *Syllabus Errorum.*
Who hasn't woken up screaming in a forest of four-poster pachyderms
where thin-skinned mahouts from their howdahs
incite us to winter in Florida?
The joint funeral of the Norwegian bareback artiste trampled by her Appaloosa
and Arachne, who fell to her death in a hippodrome in St. Louis,
reminds us no Bearded Lady nor Human Skeleton will prink
less than the Human Alligator or Missing Link
for if Jumbo succumbing to a rogue train in a marshalling yard truly marks the
     end of an era
it also truly allows us to remake ourselves as Frog Boy and the Human Chimera.

from *The American Scholar*

Word

◊ ◊ ◊

As if language could become solid.

My mother's sentences become shorter
as her needs grow smaller. And then
shorter still. Stone bridge with a diminishing

span. Become phrases. Become single
words chosen from the rubble inside
her mouth: *Bird! Outside! Water.*
Please. Tired. Tired. She has grown tired

of language. On her night stand
a tumbler of water on a plastic coaster and the last
book she ever opened in which,
for a year now, a green leather bookmark

has been holding its tongue; in which snowdrifts
on the train lines from Istanbul
have stranded Poirot just beyond Vinkovci
with twelve suspects and clues
appearing one by one—the handkerchief,
the button, the crimson kimono.

To abandon language is to stop
creating a place other than your own life
in which to live. It is to enter
the terrible certainty of the flesh. Even god
is only possible through language

but, still, I declare that it is possible
to transform a body into a temple: look

how our own lungs, unfolded
and smoothed and pressed out flat,
are the size of a spinnaker, could have a sailboat
flying before a strong wind; how they have

the dimensions of a good-sized room, a room
in which my mother might sit,
for a while, before the open window, and so enter
the heft and stance of the outside world.

I have grown used to the seethe
and abrasion of her breathing, truly. Truly.
And this is how I want to leave her, then,
my mother: in a room by an open window, turning

toward the steady compress of light
on the surface of the bay, to a skylark's rising

smear of music, and to the sleek, white pony
in the wet, roped-off pasture next door
navigating, head down, through the high

surge of wild iris to small islands
of fresh grass; as a woman
who spent the last months of her life with nothing
but rain inside her.

from *Sycamore Review*

JENI OLIN

Pillow Talk

◇   ◇   ◇

As an insomniac compulsively flips a pillow
to cool the cheek, I turn you over again & again
& again in my mind when I need the cold side
of the said affair to rail against
"the ruinous work of nostalgia."
If life imitates art, then each stillborn
has its own mucus-bright Blue Period.
Sharks keep moving to prevent dying.
People keep moving too, unwittingly staving off
the comfort of stasis, the virility of expiration, blah, blah . . .
But Death, the great highlighter, makes us all shine
a bit more dearly. I'm a widowchild who needs sunblock
against your blinding legacy. I used to get my cardio up
by just sleeping next to you. In a sane world,
I'd be bumped off to warn the others of a sky
so blue at the end of the working business day
if your veins hadn't stolen the purest
Pearl Paint blue first. A broken thoroughbred—
I need a passport & vertigo pills to reach you.
Godspeed, galloping into your Misty Blue
OMG I miss you.

from *Hanging Loose*

Cogitatio Mortis

◊   ◊   ◊

Above: the forgotten vignettes of constellations.
On the river, the ache-song of a slow thaw;
Each stone, anchored, measures the same hour.

I hitched home, which means I walked most the way.

After a while, each journey is thread spun from distance and sleet.
Moon on the pond like an open door.
After a while, each room is a waiting room.

from *New England Review*

Family Math

◇   ◇   ◇

I am more than half the age of my father,
who has lived more than twice as long
as his father, who died at thirty-six.

Once a year for four days
I am two years older than my wife,
until her birthday.

In practical terms I am three times older
than the Internet, twelve times
the age of my obsolescent computer,

eight times older than the new century
and not yet a half century old.
Impractically, here I count the nothings,

add them up to less than what I hope.
I have taught for more than half my life.
Most afternoons of teaching

follow unfinished mornings.
Yesterday I held a book seven times older
than I am. Twenty-eight hours

and a few minutes later,
I recall the smell,
a leathery, mildewed tang.

Sixteen and one-half years ago, my son
was born, which took twelve hours.
His delivery came two weeks late.

The smell in the delivery room
seemed primordial, iron in the blood,
and shit, and another kind of smell—

more abstract, if that's possible.
Twenty-six years ago I studied
abstract ideas in school, and I still don't know

what's possible. Now I teach.
My mother taught for twenty-nine years
and now she reads.

My friend remembers all he reads—
so when does he finish a book?
I can't remember when I stopped counting

on my fingers: where was I in language?
I feel older than all the wars going on,
but I'm not, some are very old.

Sadness remains the source of my politics.
In my home, very few items I own
are older than I am, and almost none I use.

We say "the wind dies down."
Is that what we mean? Lives and dies?
When babies are born, they know not

night or day. We teach them.
Tomorrow is not my birthday
but all the math will change again.

More to busy me, more to figure and record.
More to have. More to let go.

from *The Kenyon Review*

Postcards from
Her Alternate Lives

◇　◇　◇

1.

Each day the city unhinges its jaw and I climb inside.
I sing show tunes and polish its teeth. At night, I ride
its lit scales into glittered, showstopping dreams.

2.

Sister, the desert is more even than I dreamed. On each
rock rests a bowl of water, a wooden flute, a lizard.
The clouds swoop into the shape of my fears, then
blow off into the next county.

3.

I live between mountains and take my smallness,
like a pill, on waking. Always I'll be only one
more moving part, blurred in snow and stone.
I'll never fall for the slick con of consequence.

4.

Bright, or secret, or ghosted, towns fall into place
like the corner pieces of a jigsaw puzzle. All the sky
pieces look the same. I can't fit the fragments
of clouds together.

5.

This place is as I never left it: the neon sub shop
on the corner, the junior high. My house is an aquarium
filled with tulips. My mouth is a tulip filled with dust.

from *Court Green*

Horn

◊   ◊   ◊

This is the golden trophy. The true addiction.
Steel springs, pearl facings, fibers and leathers, all
Mounted on the body tarnished from neck to bell.

The master, a Legend, a "righteous addict," pauses
While walking past a bar, to listen, says: Listen—
Listen what that cat in there is doing. Some figure,

Some hook, breathy honk, sharp nine or weird
Rhythm this one back journeyman hornman had going.
Listen, says the Dante of bop, to what he's working.

Breath tempered in its chamber by hide pads
As desires and demands swarm through the deft axe
In the fixed attention of that one practitioner:

Professional calluses and habits of his righteous
Teacher, his optician. The crazed matriarch, hexed
Architect of his making. Polished and punished by use,

The horn: flawed and severe, it nestles in plush,
The hard case contoured to cradle the engraved
Hook-shape of Normandy brass, keys from seashells

In the Mekong, reed from Belize. Listen. Labor:
Do all the altered scales in the woodshed. Persist,
You practiced addict, devotee, slave of Dante

Like Dante himself a slave, whose name they say
Is short for *Durante,* meaning Persistent—listen,
Bondsman of the tool—you honker, toker, toiler.

from *New Ohio Review*

Angels

◊ ◊ ◊

They thought the job would be more musical:
Rainbows and trumpets. They'd burst
through clouds of marble streaked with flame

and offer blinding demonstrations
of the ontological proof of God.
People would look up and say "Ineffable!"

Instead, they swooped through the mall
calling *Ashley? Pammy?*
fished Mrs. Baines' wedding ring from the drain *again,*

and suspended the laws of physics on the freeway,
while simultaneously fielding the collective pleas
of Sister Perpetua's seventh grade:

Bauxite, they hiss. *Cortez. Tegucigalpa.*
Why don't they just study? one angel would gripe to another,
She *told* them Latin America would be on the test.

Gradually, they stopped showing up.
They moved into studio apartments
and took day jobs working with plants and animals.

You can spot a pair of them sometimes
at the back of the Greek diner,
giggling and whispering over fruit plates:

No, Timmy, really:
The principal export of Bolivia is lightning.
Or maybe they saunter downtown

at the end of the day, one jingling your keys, the other
tossing your lottery tickets into the gutter.
Later they'll find their way to the dark little bar

hidden away below decks,
order cocktails named after movie stars
and try out the bed in your stateroom

on a liner that left exactly on time, after all.

from *Ploughshares*

Bugcatching at Twilight

◇   ◇   ◇

A round yellow fury to the evening's light,
though ultimately it shows clemency. Shadow,

you put out your gentian-lipped goblet
and the night's lost sailors bumbled in,
a whole handful of them, squeezed into
those snug white pants.

Sorry. I mean
those were meadowhawks' wings.

You long for places you shouldn't go:
billiard halls, the pachinko palace,
behind the parked car where a Zippo flicks,
twice (sometimes you need to be summoned
twice), the places where no neon glows.

(And the *you* here is not so much you as it is I.)

I have this rearrangement to make:
symbolic death, my backward glance.
The way the past is a kind of future
leaning against the sporty hood.
On leave, he says.
He doesn't say it, but you can see it:
flattop, civvies, shirt tucked too neat.
He is so at ease, you think. You think: *at ease.*

You only have between now and o-dark-thirty.

The swift birds amass.
They, too, drawn to the buzz
hanging on the cusp of dusk.

from *The Cincinnati Review*

To my father
on the anniversary
of his death

◊   ◊   ◊

If you decide to come, bring your bouquet of
Flutes. I'll make sure the air is redolent
Of over-ripe leaves. I'll be able to walk
In heels and my mascara won't be runny. As long
As you are on your way I can sit through
The Stations of the Cross one more time, tire tracks
Through wet magnolia petals in the churchyard.
When you get here we'll watch the red
Leak into lobsters boiling on the stove, welcome
Back the luxury of butter spilling down
Our chins. If you decide to come, the roots
Of my house will stop weeping. We can pace
The widow's walk, stay up until the airport
Turns off its blue lights. In the morning
We'll drink orange juice from snifters. You can even
Doze in the long yellow grass of the abandoned
Ski slopes. However you get here, bring
Those red geraniums you say are lit from
Within. I'll finally ask how it feels
To play a pipe organ, and what you think
Happened to the old way of making friends,
Easy as laying cards down on a table.
If you decide to come we can talk it
Over. I have a balcony now where we

Can sit and flex our toes out over
The ocean, exhausted with all her little boats.

from *Post Road*

Even More Aphorisms and Ten-Second Essays from Vectors 3.0

◊　◊　◊

1.

If you can't take the first step, take the second.

2.

Experience afraid of its innocence is useless: no one is rich who cannot give his riches away.

3.

My mistakes are not mine, but they are embarrassing because you might mistake them for my sins, which are.

4.

Sophistication is upscale conformity.

5.

The days are in order, the months, the seasons, the years. But the weeks are work. They have no names; they repeat.

6.

Too much apology doubles the offense.

7.

Hard disk: the letter I remembered as embarrassing is OK after all. I must have revised it just before sending. I never confuse what I dreamed with what I actually did, but this is different: which *draft* am I?

8.

What is more yours than what always holds you back?

9.

Few plans survive their first success, which suggests they were less about their goals than about the possibility of a little success.

10.

The heart is a small, cracked cup, easy to fill, impossible to keep full.

11.

How proud we are of our multitasking. What is Life but something to get off our desks, cross off our lists?

12.

The reader lives faster than life, the writer lives slower.

13.

I need someone above me—the Committee, the Law, Money, Time—to be able to say No. Sad my lack of integrity, though I suppose it would be sadder to need them to say Yes.

14.

Self-sufficiency clings . . . to itself.

15.

If you do more than your share you'd better want to: otherwise you're paying yourself in a currency recognized nowhere else.

16.

Beware speaking of The Rich as if they were someone else.

17.

We've learned to wonder which neutralizes truth more effectively, the tyranny's censorship or the democracy's ten thousand media outlets. In the former truth is too costly, in the latter there's no market for it. In Freud the facts get around the censor in the metaphors of dreams, in Shelley we live in a dream of overfamiliarity and dead metaphor that only the poet can revivify. Does repetition emphasize or hypnotize? Which is clearer, what we see or what we don't see? Are we new or old? Do we love hate or hate love?

18.

You have two kinds of secrets. The ones only you know. The ones only you don't.

19.

The peril of arguing with you is forgetting to argue with myself. Don't make me convince you: I don't want to believe that much.

20.

Tyranny and fantasy both like to write everyone else's lines.

21.

Roadkill. Something eats the eyes first, starved for . . . what?

22.

As a couple they are salt of the earth, sodium chloride. As single elements, she was a poisonous gas and he a soft and desperate metal, turning even water into roil and flame.

23.

Don't touch, don't stare. But no one minds how hard you listen.

24.

That book, that woman, life: now that I understand them a little I realize there was something I understood better when they baffled and scared me.

25.

Nostalgia for a Lost Love. At a certain distance the parts of you and her that could never love each other become invisible, which is how you got into that whole mess in the first place.

26.

Freedom has just escaped. Peace has forgotten. Boredom is pounding on the prison gates to be let back in.

27.

It is with poetry as with love: forcing yourself is useless, you have to want to. Yet how tiresome and ungenerous is the one sprawled among flowers waiting for his impulse. There's such a thing as knowing how to make yourself want to.

28.

I'm forced to admit I'm second rate: I don't have the genius's certainty about who he is. And when I talk myself into that certainty? I'm third rate.

29.

Solitude: that home water whose sweetness you taste only when you've been someone else too long.

30.

It is the empty seats that listen most raptly.

31.

No one in human history has ever written exactly this sentence. Or anyway these two.

32.

Sure, no one's listening, English will die in a hundred years, and the far future is stones and rays. But here's the thing, you Others, you Years to Come: you do not exist.

from *The Literary Review*

What my heart is turning

◇   ◇   ◇

My heart. My heart a black flower. Not that. And is my heart an arrow
when in the morning it is crowing. My heart, my heart's crowing,
in the morning there is a blackness to the crowing of my heart.
If in the morning it wakes you. If the sky is black and then it is not
black, if the sky travels up from black and then if my heart is too loud.
My heart is awake. If my heart is awake then my heart is too loud.
If in the morning my heart is too loud and it wakes you
and your muffled eyes open and there, there is my heart in the middle
of the room. Or my heart is at the window, crowing and crowing.
Then do not touch it but watch it. So when the sky has traveled
its distance from black and then dark and then not dark and then pink,
then, when my heart has spent its restless quiver. Touch it. Touch
my heart so it burns. Turn and lean forward out of the bed, enter
the room and touch my heart like fire (this black flower, this fever,
this pitch, this scrubbed clean, this arch of morning, this riding night,
this black pitch, this fever, this book in the mouth, this bird in the city,
this siphon, this is prisoning, this fever, this pitch, this mouth
on the shelf, this bed on the back, this black city, this arch of bird,
this morning in the mouth, this woman riding night, this pitch
of fire, this bird from the prison, this shelf of fever, this back
is not clean, this arch in the chapter, this book in the morning,
this pitch, this fever, this city's on fire), be fearless, touch me
and that turning sun

from *The Iowa Review*

Provenance

◊ ◊ ◊

In the fifth grade
I made a horse of papier-mâché
and painted it white
and named it Aurora

We were all going to the hospital
each one with his little animal
to give to the girl who was
lying on her deathbed there
whose name I can't recall

A classmate with freckles perhaps
or such small feet her footsteps
never mattered much

I did not want to give her anything
It seemed unfair she got to ride Aurora
whom I made with my own two hands
and took aside at birth and said *go*
while I had to walk
perhaps for a very long time

I thought perhaps the animals
would all come back
together and on one day
but they never did

And so I have had to deal with wild
intractable people all my days

and have been led astray in a world
of shattered moonlight and beasts and trees
where no one ever even curtsies anymore
or has an understudy

So I have gone up to the little room
in my face, I am making something
out of a jar of freckles
and a jar of glue

I hated childhood
I hate adulthood
And I love being alive

from *The American Poetry Review*

Ghost Aurora

◊　◊　◊

All of the apostles, the fortune-tellers, all of those committed
to the origins of reason or faith—each is now lost in the hum

of her or his own deepening meditation. What could be the purpose
of those songs the troubadour from Avignon brought us in his leather bag?

What could be the meaning of the carvings of green falcons along
the gourd-like back of his lute? What could be more useful than a loving

principle lifted slowly out of particles, like the frond of a morning fern
uncurling? Take up your coat; take up the morning. This is what it means

to lure the phantom out of the dark, until she lifts us into the space of song.

from *Denver Quarterly* and *Poetry Daily*

The Afterlife

◇　◇　◇

*Oh shabti allotted to me, if I be summoned or if I be detailed to do any
work which has to be done in the realm of the dead . . . you shall detail
yourself for me on every occasion of making arable the fields, of flooding the
banks or conveying sand from east to west; "Here am I," you shall say.*
　　　　　　　　　　　　　　　　　　　　—The Book of the Dead

1.

They're looking a little parched
after millennia standing side
by side in the crypt, but the limestone
Egyptian couple, inseparable
on their slab, emerge from it as noble
and grand as you could ask of people
thirteen inches tall.

The pleasant, droopy-breasted wife
smiles hospitably in her gown
(the V-necked sheath "a style popular
for the entire 3,000-year
pharaonic period").
Her skin is painted paler than his:
a lady kept out of the sun.
Bare-chested in his A-line kilt,
her husband puts his spatulate
best foot forward, so as to stride
into a new life.

Not mummies; more like dummies.
Not idols, yet not merely dolls.
Stocky synecdoches
of the ruling class, they survey
an entourage of figurines
at work providing necessaries
for long days under the reigns
of dynasties still unborn.

To serenade them, here's a harpist.
A dwarf even in life—
a mascot to amuse the court
whose music must not be cut short.
A potter modeling vessels that seem,
like him, already fired in a kiln.
Six silos of wheat,
imaginary granaries.
A woman of stone grinding grain,
as she would have, on a quern of stone.
A woman winnowing grain in a pan.
Another on her knees, kneading.
A brewer mashing a vat of beer,
a butcher slitting the throat
of a heifer for the hereafter.

2.

What had it felt like, a credence
in the afterlife of art?
To die, as the departed did,
comforted by the guaranteed
incarnation of a statuette;
to feed then on that slaughtered meat?

To take a leap from the stock-still
tyranny of the literal?
To see the miniature, the fiction
as a grow-in-the-dark depiction
of the soon-to-be actual?

3.

Aboveground, thought was evolving.
So many lords and ladies died;
not everyone could be supplied
with a finely sculpted retinue
of laborers to keep them living.

And how were the high ones to keep
so many minions at their task?
The overseer with his whip
became a smiling, bland convention:
one foreman for every ten or so
farmers with a hoe.

It wasn't only math.
Something unforeseen
transforming transfiguration—
a canny, efficient faith
that less detail might well stand in
for the stand-in;
a simplicity of encryption.

Hundreds and hundreds of years passed.
Alabaster, faience, wood,
the scale of the factotum-totems
dwindled as numbers multiplied;
jostled in the mass graves
of toy-box coffins, they were transported
by a procession of living slaves
a little distance, and slipped
into their niches in the crypt
for the shelf-life of eternity.

Thumb-sized effigies wrapped
in bandages of holy script,
the hieroglyphed *Book of the Dead.*

Words. The nominal vow to work,
not the enactment of work.

The *shabti* held one stylized tool,
barely identifiable—
and were serene as Christian saints
with their hatchets and wheels, the instruments
of a recurring martyrdom.
In time they grew more mummiform,
cross-armed at the chest
or armless. Finally, curiously, at rest—

like zeroes who were something
in being nothing,
place-markers of their own
as much as of the master's soul.

4.

And on the wall of a vault,
an artist has drawn himself—
or a cunning substitute—
at work, shaping a life-sized *shabti*
designed to be his twin:
a goateed dandy that our mute,
vainglorious ventriloquist
settles on one knee.

Profile to profile, they stare
into the mannered mirror
of the other.

In whatever kingdom this was
(by now, the blink
of one kohl-lined, almond eye),
what did people think was the lifespan
of the stunt man who betokens man?
The *shabti* sent to make *shabti*?

But the question too has shrunken,
eroded to vocabulary—
one fine old potsherd of a word

to be carried from the museum
like any other item
in the museum shop:
a replica necklace, a postcard.

The visitor is illiterate.
What did that stone scroll say,
meant to convert someday
to the thing it represents, papyrus?
Even the scribes couldn't read.
Something about the god Osiris
who came back from the dead.

She must be going.
Feels for the gloves in her pockets,
empty hands for her hands.

Opens a door to Chicago,
where a fine dust is ticking
coldly onto everything;
where she is still alive, and it's snowing.

from *Southwest Review*

JAMES SCHUYLER

The Smallest

◇   ◇   ◇

It is in front of the tree.
The houses around the windows are lit
by it, it turns off and goes upon
knees and wherever the bone is almost next
to the skin. It has been defamed.
It will become undernourished.
It is not without end. It is not.
It is not what you can let happen,
or cause to happen, or has anything
at all to do with happening.
It happens as it exists without effect.
It is the pure in pure mathematics.
It is the sully in unsullied rain.
It is the pain in painfully.
It is also the fully. It is
the light in highlight and headlight,
the head in headland, the towering
in towers, trees, the outstretched
in shadows of mountains on plains and lakes.
It is not the water in the lake, however,
it is not cupped.
If it exists, it is unaware of it.
It could name itself however, and does.
It contains alphabets.
It is infinite and therefore the smallest thing.

from *The Nation*

Nineteen Thirty-Eight

◊   ◊   ◊

That was the year the Nazis marched into Vienna,
Superman made his debut in Action Comics,
Stalin was killing off his fellow revolutionaries,
The first Dairy Queen opened in Kankakee, Ill.,
As I lay in my crib peeing in my diapers.

"You must have been a beautiful baby," Bing Crosby sang.
A pilot the newspapers called Wrong Way Corrigan
Took off from New York heading for California
And landed instead in Ireland, as I watched my mother
Take a breast out of her blue robe and come closer.

There was a hurricane that September causing a movie theater
At Westhampton Beach to be lifted out to sea.
People worried the world was about to end.
A fish believed to have been extinct for seventy million years
Came up in a fishing net off the coast of South Africa.

I lay in my crib as the days got shorter and colder,
And the first heavy snow fell in the night.
Making everything very quiet in my room.
I believe I heard myself cry for a long, long time.

from *The Paris Review*

Nowhere

◇　◇　◇

i.m. Steve Sigur

The sprinkler system wakes up on the hour,
sprawling in vacant arcs across the lawn.
All night its clockwork tends to every flower
bedded down here to bury roots and spawn
while, nowhere in particular, my friend
who just last week lay mumbling on a cot
is dead, is nothing time or work can mend,
though his machinery remains, to rot
as I walk late at night across a campus
hundreds of miles away, which is to say
as near to him as anywhere, and *tempus
fugit* no less *irreparabile*
from me than from the blossoms here and there
who do not know their lot, and do not care.

from *Iron Horse Literary Review*

PATRICIA SMITH

Motown Crown

◊   ◊   ◊

The Temps, all swerve and pivot, conjured schemes
that had us skipping school, made us forget
how mamas schooled us hard against the threat
of five-part harmony and sharkskin seams.
We spent our schooldays balanced on the beams
of moon we wished upon, the needled jet-
black 45s that spun and hadn't yet
become the dizzy spinning of our dreams.
Sugar Pie, Honey Bun, oh you
loved our nappy hair and rusty knees.
Marvin Gaye slowed down while we gave chase
and then he was our smokin' fine taboo.
We hungered for the anguished screech of *Please*
inside our chests—relentless, booming bass.

ℰ ℭ

Inside our chests, relentless booming bass
softened to the turn of Smokey's key.
His languid, liquid, luscious, aching plea
for bodies we didn't have yet made a case
for lying to ourselves. He could erase
our bowlegs, raging pimples, we could see
his croon inside our clothes, his pedigree
of milky flawless skin. Oh, we'd replace
our *daddies* with his fine and lanky frame,
I did you wrong, my heart went out to play
he serenaded, filling up the space
that separated Smoke from certain flame.

We couldn't see the drug of him—OK,
silk where his throat should be. He growled such grace.

කා ශ

Silk where his throat should be, and growling grace,
Little Stevie made us wonder why
we even *needed* sight. His rhythm eye
could see us click our hips and swerve in place
whenever *he* cut loose. Ooh, we'd unlace
our Converse All-Stars. Yeah, we wondered why
we couldn't get down *without* our shoes, we'd try
and dance and keep up with his funky pace
of hiss and howl and hum, and then he'd slow
to twist our hearts until he heard them crack,
ignoring what was leaking from the seams.
The rockin' blind boy couldn't help but show
us light. We bellowed every soulful track
from open window, 'neath the door—pipe dreams.

කා ශ

From open windows, 'neath the doors, pipe dreams
taught us bone, bouffant and nicotine
and served up Lady D, the boisterous queen
of overdone, her body built from beams
of awkward light. Her bug-eyed brash extremes
dizzied normal girls. The evergreen
machine, so clean and mean, dabbed kerosene
behind our ears and said *Now burn.* Our screams
meant only that our hips would now be thin,
that we'd hear symphonies, wouldn't hurry love,
as Diana said, *Make sure it gleams
no matter what it is.* Her different spin,
a voice like sugar air, no inkling of
a soul beneath the vinyl. The Supremes.

කා ශ

That soul beneath the vinyl, the Supremes
knew nothing of it. They were breathy sighs
and fluid hips, soul music's booby prize.
But Mary Wells, so drained of self-esteem,
was a pudgy, barstool-ridin' buck-toothed dream
who none of us would dare to idolize
out loud. She had our mamas' grunt and thighs
and we preferred to just avoid THAT theme—
as well as war and God and gov'ment cheese
and bullets in the street and ghetto blight.
While Mary's "My Guy" blared, we didn't think race,
'cause there was all that romance, and the keys
that Motown held. Unlocked, we'd soon ignite.
We stockpiled extra sequins, just in case.

ஐ ෬

We stockpiled extra sequins, just in case
the Marvelettes decided that our grit
was way beyond Diana's, that we fit
inside their swirl, a much more naughty place.
Those girls came from the brick, we had to brace
ourselves against their heat, much too legit
to dress up as some other thing. We split
our blue jeans trying to match their pace.
And soon our breasts commenced to pop, we spoke
in deeper tones, and Berry Gordy looked
and licked his lips. Our only saving grace?
The luscious, liquid languid tone of Smoke,
the soundtrack while our A-cup bras unhooked.
Our sudden Negro hips required more space.

ஐ ෬

Our sudden Negro hips required more space,
but we pretended not to feel that spill
that changed the way we walked. And yes, we still
couldn't help but feel so strangely out of place
while Motown filled our eager hearts with lace
and Valentines. Romance was all uphill,

119

no push, no prod, no shiny magic pill
could lift us to that light. No breathing space
in all that time. We grew like vines to sun,
and then we burned. As mamas shook their heads
and mourned our Delta names, we didn't deem
to care. Religion—there was only one.
We took transistor preachers to our beds
and Smokey sang a lyric dripping cream.

℘ ℭ

While Smokey sang a lyric dripping cream,
Levi tried to woo us with his growl:
Can't help myself. Admitted with a scowl,
his bit of weakness was a soulful scheme—
and we kept screaming, front row, under gleam
of lights, beside the speakers' blasting vowels,
we rocked and screamed. Levi, on the prowl,
glowed black, a savior in the stagelight's beam.
But then the stagelight dimmed, and there we were
in bodies primed—for what we didn't know.
We sang off-key while skipping home alone.
Deceptions that you sing to tend to blur
and disappear in dance, why is that so?
Ask any colored girl and she will moan.

℘ ℭ

Ask any colored girl and she will moan
an answer with a downbeat and a sleek
five-part croon. She's dazzled, and she'll shriek
what she's been taught: She won't long be alone,
or crazed with wanting more. One day she'll own
that quiet heart that Motown taught to speak,
she'll know that being the same makes her unique.
She'll rest her butt on music's paper throne
until the bassline booms, until some old
Temptation leers and says *I'll take you home
and heal you in the way the music vowed.*

She's trapped within his clutch, his perfumed hold,
dancing to his conjured, crafted poem,
remembering how. Love had lied so loud.

℘ ℭ

Remembering how love had lied so loud,
we tangled in the rhythms that we chose.
Seduced by thump and sequins, heaven knows
we tried to live our looming lives unbowed,
but bending led to break. We were so proud
to mirror every lyric. Radios
spit beg and mend, and precious stereos
told us what we were and weren't allowed.
Our daddies sweat in factories while we
found other daddies under limelight's glow.
And then we begged those daddies to create
us. Like Stevie, help us blindly see
the rhythms, but instead, the crippling blow.
We whimpered while the downbeat dangled bait.

℘ ℭ

We whimpered while the downbeat dangled bait,
we leapt and swallowed all the music said
while Smokey laughed and Marvin idly read
our minds and slapped us hard and slapped us straight,
and even then, we listened for the great
announcement of the drum, for tune to spread,
a Marvelette to pick up on the thread.
But as we know by now, it's much too late
to reconsider love, or claw our way
through all the glow they tossed to slow our roll.
What we know now we should have always known.
When Smokey winked at us and then said *They
don't love you like I do,* he snagged our soul.
We wound up doing the slow drag, all alone.

℘ ℭ

They made us do the slow drag, all alone.
They made us kiss our mirrors, deal with heat,
our bodies sudden bumps. They danced deceit
and we did too, addicted to the drone
of revelation, all the notes they'd thrown
our way: *Oh, love will change your life. The sweet*
sweet fairy tale we spin will certainly beat
the real thing any day. Oh, yes we own
you now. We sang you pliable and clue-
less, waiting, waiting, oh the dream you'll hug
one day, the boy who craves you right out loud
in front of everyone. But we told you,
we know we did, we preached it with a shrug—
less than perfect love was not allowed.

₧ ₨

Less than perfect love was not allowed.
Temptations begged as if their every sway
depended on you coming home to stay.
Diana whispered air, aloof and proud
to be the perfect girl beneath a shroud
of glitter and a fright she held at bay.
And Michael Jackson, flailing in the fray
of daddy love, succumbed to every crowd.
What would we have done if not for them,
wooing us with roses carved of sound
and hiding muck we're born to navigate?
Little did we know that they'd condemn
us to live so tethered to the ground.
While every song they sang told us to wait.

₧ ₨

Every song they sang told us to wait
and wait we did, our gangly heartbeats stunned
and holding place. Already so outgunned
we little girls obeyed. And now it's late,
and CDs spinning only help deflate
us. The songs all say, *Just look what you've done,*

you've wished through your whole life. And one by one
your stupid sisters boogie to their fate.
So now, at fifty plus, I turn around
and see the glitter drifting in my wake
and mingling with the dirt. My dingy dreams
are shoved high on the shelf. They're wrapped and bound
so I can't see and contemplate the ache.
The Temps, all swirl and pivot, conjured schemes.

℘ ℭ

The Temps, all swirl and pivot, conjured schemes
inside our chests, relentless booming bass
then silk where throats should be. Much growling grace
from open window, 'neath the door, pipe dreams—
that soul beneath the vinyl. The Supremes
used to stockpile extra sequins just in case
Diana's Negro hips required more space,
while Smokey penned a lyric dripping cream.
Ask any colored girl, and she will moan,
remembering how love had lied so loud.
I whimpered while the downbeat dangled bait
and taught myself to slow drag, all alone.
Less than perfect love was not allowed
and every song they sang told me to wait.

from *Rattle*

Dream IV

◇　◇　◇

I am so laden I grieve at 3 A.M.
over two parking spaces I could have claimed
or am fully frightened in a basement room choosing
a Nobel laureate among the nine Israelis
upstairs, especially when their phone call says
you don't have anything to be frightened of; nor would
I choose a Jubu, nor would I choose someone
with a ring in her tongue for it says in Numbers that
tin coated with silver is against the law
of mixing metals, such as we can't cook peppers
in a steel pot for steel is what we put
in a horse's mouth and what we make swords of
by dipping iron in oxide in the first place,
though it was no accident deliberately tipping wood
or fusing, as they did, Jewish and German
genius and German and Jewish chemicals
underground, and in the desert, I say fuck you
to fusion and I say let them fight with iron,
better with bronze, or better yet with wood,
or air, oh let them fight with air, drop air
from B100s, consider it, Kissinger.

from *The New Yorker*

Pantoum
for the Imperceptible

◊   ◊   ◊

Germs talked me into it.
　　　It was the parable that talked me out.
Behold I stood in the furious garden, counterfeit
　　　with my fingers in the ground.

It was the parable that talked me out.
My cells told me what to do.
　　　Said, go put your fingers in the ground.
So I planted tomatoes and thyme for you.

It was my cells that told me what to do.
This is my reckless psalm.
　　　Venomous nightshades and time on you;
my dog was alive and my hair was long.

This is another reckless psalm.
My body was stubborn as green oak wood;
　　　My dog was alive, my hair was long,
we slept on the porch when the wind was good,

but I was stubborn as green oak wood.
　　　Now I am stuck with the imperceptible lovers.
I sleep on the porch when the wind is good.
　　　Neither of us live without the other,

so I am stuck with these imperceptible lovers.
　　　It is spring and I am capable of anything.

I live without the other.
    My body trembles with memory,

knowing is it spring, capable of anything.
    Is it true I am never alone?
My body trembles with memory.
    It is not piety, but this that pulls me home—

It is true, I am never alone
    in the garden, furious and counterfeit.
It was not piety, but this that pulled me home.
    It was germs who talked me into it.

from *Maggy*

The Poem
of the Spanish Poet

◊ ◊ ◊

In a hotel room somewhere in Iowa an American poet, tired of his poems, tired of being an American poet, leans back in his chair and imagines he is a Spanish poet, an old Spanish poet, nearing the end of his life, who walks to the Guadalquivir and watches the ships, gray and ghostly in the twilight, slip downstream. The little waves, approaching the grassy bank where he sits, whisper something he can't quite hear as they curl and fall. Now what does the Spanish poet do? He reaches into his pocket, pulls out a notebook, and writes:

> Black fly, black fly
> Why have you come
>
> Is it my shirt
> My new white shirt
>
> With buttons of bone
> Is it my suit
>
> My dark blue suit
> Is it because
>
> I lie here alone
> Under a willow
>
> Cold as stone
> Black fly, black fly

How good you are
To come to me now

How good you are
To visit me here

Black fly, black fly
To wish me goodbye

from *Salmagundi*

Thirteen Months

◊ ◊ ◊

April

I did consider the Blue Book value
against airbags, the other trade-offs: no
sunroof, loose bumper, tilt-back lever jammed.
Got the title, fair speed in general—and just
one concession, a speed bump's tenderness.
I have to thank the shocks, and certain thrills
out on the open road: tail-fires blasting
out the carbon, the license to stop or cross
the tracks and shriek. Other top features:
full blasts of heat, salt-damaged chrome,
two roll-down windows, at least one headlight
to track the sun back home. Dings. I hated
this marriage, damaged slowly beyond repair,
though I thrilled at rides that blew back my hair.

May 7 (your birthday)

For eighteen years we drove to your parents
through smog from steel mills and rivers
converging, the swift Connoquenessing,
the Slippery Rock. But they'd bulldozed
the ovens down, girders and rust melted
away, a graveyard where you once smelted
stainless tubes, ablaze, dark eyes smoldering.
Across from Loccisano's Grocery,
that ash hopper for dumping chemicals,

slag, where you and your cousins lobbed footballs,
snowballs: grace and iron. You held on to those
plays, kept your aim to forge raw elements
into enduring forms, choreographed
a life's dream that the mill would send you on.

Memorial Day

A in *alone* is a sound known as schwa—
a slight *uh* we make with our tongue low and level,
a common hum. In old Hebrew schwa stood
for letters not noted. Schwa, written *e,*
but upside down—remember? You probably
learned it on a first-grade chart. But that's not
important. It's how schwa is spoken: just pretend
that I'm listening for your admiration,
for an unstressed *us.* I'm all anticipation, wet lips
barely open, then out your mouth it runs:
uh, uh—*affair*—your schwa, so ancient and
correctly pronounced, far back in the throat.
Say it again: *affair, affair*—now more
smoothly. Watch the syllabification.

July

Black soil over an ancient privy pit
where I must dig out clay chips. They threaten
the delphinium. I wonder who once
flung garbage into what is now garden.
Whole nuts, nit combs, buttons and pins, fragments
of lamp float up now and again. And this,
another pentimento: blue cobalt
tattoo of nightingale, without saucer
companion, soaring still on a cup's cracked
skin. Repented belongings that turn up
like runes, talisman discovered, taken
for woe. The time was when I didn't think

it odd to find a perfume stopper or
entertain the question it was raising.

November 11

Instructions for a plague: Burn entrails.
Always check the pulse with gaze turned away.
Obtain ring finger knuckles. Gather shirt,
apron, handkerchief. Squeeze vinegar through
or taint stays. Turn mirrors for protection.
Poultice thigh to trunk. For disinfection,
forget not bud roses nor herbs with strong
perfume. From solstice to the equinox
scatter blood meal. All this doth wring a cure.
Or flee. Sing, laugh, indulge every new
appetite. Choose finest sweetmeats, drink dry
wine, but temperately. Collect whatnots,
dulcet hours for hunting, dance, and suchlike
pleasures. When the sick fall, show them the stones.

December

I take the children bowling, yes, in hopes
that at the alley a little disco
bumps my heart, and if they turn the black lights
on and each pin glows, I can somehow gauge
the angles right, find the velocity
that knocks ten pins down. Silhouettes, neon
lights, rows and rows of worn black balls on shelves,
the shuttlecocks, young foosballers and league
bowlers times twelve, all of us hefting weight
to fling and slide, then wait, genuflecting
on one knee, all the right body English
imploring a strike, that resounding sound.
Christmas is next week. I'll be alone. Our
kids, your new girlfriend, will be with you.

February

Our children believe you when you say you'll live.
I hear you're wasting—you've lost sixty pounds.
From that crest of hill above the train yard
they're gliding down on their plastic Christmas
sleds, not too far from where the 280 bridge
straightens highway, combs train tracks to the ground.
Maybe twenty detached coal cars tonight
wait to hook up, load up, full again.
The distant overhead billboard says,
#1 silent killer? Depression.
The kids bring up other things. Their mittened
fingers' burning cold. That they toe the hill,
don't fall down. In a film at school some Bronze Age
man dug from a bog, skin and bone.

April 1

Breath in blooms, I cover new flowerbeds
in blankets. They're forecasting cold like pox.
Now the garden too becomes a hospice
and we'll likely see a spring killer frost.
As for death, we just delay the petals.
Doctors steep you in treatment, your mother
says her beads. Do you care they've made a priest
your accountant? Does he keep his raven's
scorecard of your soul? Do you give a lot
of thought to contrition? Arithmetic?
You'll see now what's behind the sliding door.
I haven't kept good faith or religion.
For this—contrition. Try to pardon me.
What can I add but flowers for the bier?

April 15

Aida, sharp and sweet as blood oranges
that young spring in Verona when you

led me to market, palmed a few lira
for stained labels: the village wine. Nearby
in a meat stall the butcher's knife opened
a stunned hare. He peeled off the skin, seized
the cardinal organs, the scarlet liver slid.
A clot with its syrup clinging, it filled
a small bowl. Today doctors call. We hurry.
You hold up a plastic bag, say: *Contents*
of my stomach. Are you impressed? Then our
daughter runs shrieking from your room. More bags
hang ungenerously from metal hooks,
silently ensure the coming encores.

Late April

You said *yes.* A secret was the twisted
part of you, and shame, in the end a debt
your body had been mortgaged to. The cost
of losing face—an organ turned to pus?
A slowly slaughtered faith, trust wormed through.
What couldn't wait, or last. You said *young,* and
young, you'd seen the lake. Why had you never
guessed that it kept from you its source, its depth,
how it looked at you and loved? Weeping
made the water cloud, lust the hidden ledge.
Reflected, the light from your abdomen,
the margins—of you, of us—changed just at
the end, your own face floating up, hopeful
lines, tubes, serum. *No,* your mouth and eyes said.

End of April

We were all leaving our bodies—but no
one helped us, no one said, *Breathe into*
the spaces you can't feel. We were all losing
our bearings. We'd seen you, Vesuvian, you
who grasped any hand to crush it inside yours,
voice rasping out: *See how strong I am!* and

133

your will greater than chemo. Do you
agree it was your plan all along, your brand
of curative violence—mind's NO versus
body's letting go? How funny, dying,
you didn't remember this: on a mountain,
years ago, you'd encountered a vision. You
would die young. You never got sick of your
body. It kept you as long as it could.

Early May

Vermivora peregrina, pilgrim
warbler, old devotee of maggot grub
and upturned stump, mossy hummock lover,
ace catcher—who yes, slyly, took to branch,
snatched an insect then glanced around—*seet,
seet, seet*—and flew. Little molter, just
back from Panama this glazed May to make
your northern nest, ever the mover, straggler
from scrub, thicket breeder, builder of dome
from the hair of moose, fine moss, quill and here
in the city where larvae crawl trash cans,
dead. Near glass, one olive-gray handful.
Nothing sullied except your black eyes drying,
worm-eating pilgrim I rescue from worms.

May 7

What choice was there but to layer pancake
makeup deep, his undertaker cousin
says. Chemo mixed with embalming fluid
could work like that. My husband, eighteen
years, my children's father, laid out wearing
three of his father's shirts at once, and still
looking small in his casket. We all sob.
Up close we see through thin hair to green scalp.
I touch his chest, once barrel-shaped. Beneath
my hand the rib he broke the first time I

saw him on stage, a night *Newsweek* reviewed,
singling out his Drosselmeyer, to his delight:
" . . . an unusual reading of the role—
like Clark Gable crossed with Dracula."

from *Beloit Poetry Journal*

Elegy

◊   ◊   ◊

for my father

I think by now the river must be thick
     with salmon. Late August, I imagine it

as it was that morning: drizzle needling
     the surface, mist at the banks like a net

settling around us—everything damp
     and shining. That morning, awkward

and heavy in our hip waders, we stalked
     into the current and found our places—

you upstream a few yards, and out
     far deeper. You must remember how

the river seeped in over your boots,
     and you grew heavy with that defeat.

All day I kept turning to watch you, how
     first you mimed our guide's casting,

then cast your invisible line, slicing the sky
     between us; and later, rod in hand, how

you tried—again and again—to find
     that perfect arc, flight of an insect

skimming the river's surface. Perhaps
        you recall I cast my line and reeled in

two small trout we could not keep.
        Because I had to release them, I confess,

I thought about the past—working
        the hooks loose, the fish writhing

in my hands, each one slipping away
        before I could let go. I can tell you now

that I tried to take it all in, record it
        for an elegy I'd write—one day—

when the time came. Your daughter,
        I was that ruthless. What does it matter

if I tell you I *learned* to be? You kept casting
        your line, and when it did not come back

empty, it was tangled with mine. Some nights,
        dreaming, I step again into the small boat

that carried us out and watch the bank receding—
        my back to where I know we are headed.

from *New England Review*

Drunk at a Party

◇   ◇   ◇

He couldn't imagine it now,
kicking back, back kicking,
wandering around with a glass,
weirdly morose or—what's the word?—
jolly. His voice sounding vaguely Swiss
or Peruvian or Dutch. Could he
pick up the rhythm
of the lush he once was,
get lugubrious with that woman
from the controller's office?
Break down, regret everything or—
the opposite—
boast? What latch keeps a brain
from spinning like a prawn
dropped on a stranger's parquet?
Ages ago in a land far away
lucky people got three martinis for lunch.
Whole lifetimes hung on a ledge
disgorging the slippery
feelers of sloe gin.
Who would he be
if he passed out again?
Or if love plucked his eyes
and made any throat glisten?
This descendant of men who broke
their necks
in buckets of hard cider?
Why am I speaking
at this moment

as if I were a man?
What ruse am I guilty of?
What keeps a lobster out of a tank?

from *AGNI*

Thoreau and the Lightning

◊   ◊   ◊

The white ash tree, the one he'd visited
    time after time and season after season
and had studied and admired like a proud father,
    had been struck by lightning. Lightning
had gouged downward, tossing broken limbs
    every which way, had split the trunk
into six twenty-foot splayed, upstanding fence rails
    still held up by the roots, had plowed a furrow
into a cellar (where it scorched the milk pans),
    had bolted out in a shower of soil, had shattered
weatherboards and beams and the foundation,
    had smashed a shed, unstacked and scattered a woodpile,
had flung pieces of bark two hundred feet
    in all directions. It had thrown into disorder
or destroyed in a moment what an honest farmer
    had struggled for years to gather, and had killed
a great tree. Was he supposed to be humbled
    by the benign, malign, inscrutable purposes
of the Source, the blundering Maker of Thunderheads,
    and give thanks he hadn't been standing under it?

from *Ecotone*

The Latch

◇　◇　◇

After scraping eighty-three-year-old paint from four screw heads
holding the latch in place on the studio door,
and, having steadied the door on one out-thrust hip and running
the pointed tip of a kitchen knife around the lock-box to break the seal

of paint, your neighbor patiently removed each screw with the right-size,
old-fashioned screwdriver he had brought and jiggled the lock free
so he could pry open its metal back and fish out the broken spring,
the small, dark, steel coil and its detached tongue,

which could be replaced, he thought, by an antiquarian locksmith
on the other side of town in la rue du Courreau—
though the latch will be too late to keep in or out
the man who abandoned this house, and the good and ill spirits he courted here.

from *The Atlantic*

Time Pieces

◇　◇　◇

Eden time

They spent every day,
blissfully ignorant, in
amorous delay.

Temp time

Will I be alive
when the twelve-headed jailer
announces it's five?

In a parched time

Clouds make this appeal:
the more you wait, the wetter
the water will feel.

Intermission time

Guilty admission:
this plunge from art to life's a
painful transition.

Sleep time

Quick nap—but it seemed
an ocean of joys, a sea
of griefs that I dreamed.

Reunion time

Days passed like drugged snails.
I met you at the station,
laughed at their faint trails.

Just give it time

Though I frankly feel
better, there's nothing sadder
than starting to heal.

Retronym time

Cheering: it was done.
But soon the Great War would be
renamed World War One.

Lately I haven't had the easiest time

Overcathexis
has me asking clouds if they
know where my ex is.

The Marschallin returns for the third and final time

Ja, ja, so it goes:
I've got memories, but she's
got the silver rose.

Ahab time

Though I do not thrive,
I confess I've never felt
so purely alive.

You get lucky from time to time

Once, in a mad rush,
I painted a blizzard that
blew away my brush.

from *The New Criterion*

Ecclesiastes II:I

◇　◇　◇

We must *cast our bread*
Upon the waters, as the
Ancient preacher said,

Trusting that it may
Amply be restored to us
After many a day.

That old metaphor,
Drawn from rice farming on the
River's flooded shore,

Helps us to believe
That it's no great sin to give,
Hoping to receive.

Therefore I shall throw
Broken bread, this sullen day,
Out across the snow,

Betting crust and crumb
That birds will gather, and that
One more spring will come.

from *The New Yorker*

C . K . W I L L I A M S

A Hundred Bones

◊   ◊   ◊

In this mortal frame of mine, which is made of a hundred bones and nine orifices,
there is something, and this something can be called, for lack of a better name, a
windswept spirit . . .

—Bashō

And thus the hundred bones of my body plus various apertures plus that thing
    I don't know yet
to call spirit are all aquake with joyous awe at the shriek of the fighter planes that
    from their base
at Port Newark swoop in their practice runs so low over our building that the
    walls tremble.

Wildcats, they're called, *Thunderbolts* or *Corsairs,* and they're practicing *strafing,*
    which in war means
your machine guns are going like mad as you dive down on the enemy soldiers
    and other bad people,
Nips, Krauts, trying to run out from under your wings, your bullet-pops leaping
    after their feet.

It's a new word for us, *strafing.* We learn others, too: *blockbusters,* for instance,
    which means
bombs that smash down your whole block: not our block, some *Nip* block, or
    Nazi—
some gray block in the newsreel. B-24 is the number of my favorite bomber:
    the *Liberator.*

My best fighter: *Lightning.* The other kind of lightning once crashed on an eave
    of our building
and my mother cried out and swept me up in her arms: *The war is here,* she must
    have thought,

146

the war has found me. All her life I think she was thinking: *The war is here, the war has found me.*

Some words we don't know yet—*gas chamber, napalm*—children our age, in nineteen forty-four, say,
say Arnold Lilien and I, who're discussing how we'll torture our treacherous enemy-friends
who've gone off to a ball game without us. They're like enemies, Japs or Nazis: so of course torture.

Do children of all places and times speak so passionately and knowledgeably about torture?
Our imaginations are small, though, Arnold's and mine. Tear out their nails. Burn their eyes.
Drive icicles in their ear so there's no evidence of your having done it except they're dead.

Then it was Arnold who died. He was a doctor; out West; he learned to fly "Piper Cubs,"
and flew out to help Navajo women have babies. He'd become a good man. Then he was dead.
But right now: victory! V-Day! Clouds like giant ice creams over the evil Japanese empire.

Cities are burning. Some Japanese cities aren't even there. *The war is here! The war has found me!*
Japanese poets come later. We don't know we need them until they're already buffing the lens.
Bashō. Issa. Buson. Especially Bashō: ah, that *windswept spirit;* ah, that hardly there frog.

Atom bomb, though: Bashō as shadow burned into asphalt. House torn by mad burning wind.
Poets in coats of straw, burning. What is our *flaw,* we human-beings? What is our *error?*
Spikes in your tushy, ice in your brain. That frog invisibly waiting forever to make its leap.

from *AGNI*

Mix Tape to Be Brought to Her in Rehab

◊ ◊ ◊

Black lacquered circle & the sound coaxed
   from diamond to rest within the acetate glimmer,
      the agon & the joys commingling. Nina Simone

is conjuring The Boat of Ra Little Darling
   from a long cold lonely winter, though outside
      it is August & is not all right. Double doors,

then again double doors. You will sign yourself in:
   & they'll rifle your bag of oranges & candy bars,
      pry open the plastic case & hold the gray

Maxell against the light. Immense are the tears
   of Levi Stubbs. How sweet how sweet the honeybee.
      The Smiths are in a terrible place. O Oscillate

Wildly Please Please Please Let Me Get What I Want,
   to be followed in turn by Mr. James Brown,
      his own pleas trembling the Apollo rafters.

Visiting hours—in the TV room the Haldol reigns.
   The President struts among the SS gravestones,
      pompadour shiny as a new LP, his movie-actor gait

turned thank God to pastel vapor by *Miami Vice*.
Flamingos starburst from the credits. Shyly
she will walk the corridor to meet you, your offerings

of Earl Grey, the two black turtlenecks.
Nails cobalt—fingers a-tremble. Gun Shy, Screaming
Blue Messiahs, Dylan at his nadir adenoiding

Brownsville Girl—*down here even the swap meets
are getting a little corr-rupt*. Richard Thompson
When the Spell Is Broken, Jimmy Cliff's

in limbo waiting for the dice to roll.
When her roommate leaves, you'll sit with her upon the bed.
Awkward you will small-talk, staring

at your hands. More doors, double doors & triple,
the years the years. Down the carved names
the future with its labyrinths & tailspins, rooms

giving way to rooms, the upturned car, the notebooks
cuneiformed with numbers, pivot & gyre, cache
of Rx pads stuffed into a rolltop drawer. 90 rabid

troubled minutes, coda Robert Johnson. Stones on my
passway & my road seem dark as night. Her eyes in memory
an astonished blue. You reach inside your jacket

& she holds it in her upturned palm. From the bedside
table she lifts the Walkman—the button with its triangle,
the click, the whir, the eddying forward.

from *Prairie Schooner*

Toadstools

◇   ◇   ◇

The toadstools are starting to come up,
                           circular and dry.
Nothing will touch them,
Gophers or chipmunks, wasps or swallows.
They glow in the twilight like rooted will-o'-the-wisps.
Nothing will touch them.
As though little roundabouts from the bunched unburiable,
Powers, dominions,
As though orphans rode herd in the short grass,
                           as though they had heard the call,
They will always be with us,
                      transcenders of the world.
Someone will try to stick his beak into their otherworldly styrofoam.
Someone may try to taste a taste of forever.
For some it's a refuge, for some a shady place to fall down.
Grief is a floating barge-boat,
                      who knows where it's going to moor?

from *The New Yorker*

STEPHEN YENSER

Cycladic Idyll: An Apologia

◊   ◊   ◊

I don't know why you don't just go over to Catalina.
                                        —Bill Edinger

1

I come here for the views.

I come because there is no news.

Because things have been arranged. Because I have no other plans.
    Because there are no plans for me. Because I do not have to
    choose.

I come here for the arid, aromatic, aromantic emptiness—where one might
    "get a grip" and "sort things out." Add them up. Make some
    sum. Compose oneself—like a concerto for flute and strings.

I come to be alone. Because I am alone. Out of season. Like the few
    midges left. Adrift on a stony island no known poet hails from.
    Enisled. Outlandish as that term. (*Annihiled* is different but only
    by a smidge.)

To remind myself how simple things can be. Simple as the music of the
    marble figures of the harpist—and the unique double-reed player.

Not to mention concepts. To remind myself how when it comes to things
    like concepts, Heraclitus and Plato had all we would ever need.
    (Pythagoras I set aside for now.)

I come here to learn to speak clearly. To make carefully with the right
     mouthparts the sounds for *thing* and *nothing,* for *bread* and *wine,*
     for *come* and *go, here* and *now* and *then* and *there.* For *good*
     evening and *farewell.*

Because my own language has become extravagant and tra-la, tra-la.
     Tralatitious, one might say. And—the olives everywhere remind
     me—indecently indehiscent.

Because I want fewer such words to weigh. To be less weighword, so to
     say. Therefore less wayward and less spendthrift. Less spindrift,
     in a word.

Not to mention grave, preponderant, and dark. (I come here to be struck
     by *lightening!*)

Because here in the right place a *thésis* can be a good flat stone to sit on
     and not a lizardlike thing to nail down then argue with.

Because here amid abandoned villages' abundant dilapidation there is no
     reason for reason, no urge to originality.

Because as I wait to be transported by the bus I read on small trucks that
     ply the main road the descriptor *Metaphorá.*

I come here to sit at length and read some Whitman, who adored words
     plain as stones, regardless of those exultant exaltations of
     "eidolons."

To browse idly, to idle on in a brief, worn lexicon, to let it lead me on.

Because I need new old sayings. Because the good ones die too soon.
     Because bean by bean fills the bag.

Because I will save time, because it will not save me, here where it twists
     on itself like the walkways to waylay laid-up freebooters like me
     and my dead friend.

2

I come back to stop in on the way to see this time by appointment Edward
Lear's watercolors in the Gennadius,

Because he did them as sketches for oils he could paint then sell back
home, so they were valueless themselves, so they were kept
unmatted and loose in cartons pulled off shelves thirty years ago
for improvident visitors like me and my friend who was my guide
to shuffle through and take quick notes like these on his.

Because even this delicate, vehicular medium meant fixity, his
nemesis, so in hopes that glazed and scumbled oils could get the
shifty shades right, he jotted in light pencil across the images
descriptions, shot through with nonce terms and puns fleeting as
pains taken, rubbed and faded, sometimes indecipherable, wishful
notes written on washes disappearing before our eyes, which
follow them, into sea, cliff, olive stand, distant temple, dovecote,
asphodel.

"catch gold light grass"   "all turquoisy & Byzantine bluesy"   "O
poppies!"   "very olivish"

3

I come here not to contemn my city's columbaria of condominiums and
book emporia with their stacks of fresh books on chocolate
chockablock with guides to the Galápagos and *Godot* and their
tables laden with books on coffee tables and books on coffee-table
books,

And not to malign the midnight supermarkets' own tropic aisles, with their
tanned and juicy, shrink-wrapped dates, their bruise-ripe figs
burnished by gelled lights (O psychedelicacies!) and the racks of
razors and glossy magazines and analgesics.

I come not to ditch the academy's deliciously multiplicious *pharmakon,*
though disembarking I accidentally dropped into the sea my
faithful Dopp kit, full of the life-saving medicines that took it

down, perhaps as it chose, since it seemed to leap from my hand
through an opening just its size.

I come here to address not deconstruction but myself.

To address myself to the oregano (a whiff on the breeze nostalgic and
heady as skunk) cropping up beside the ubiquitous retaining walls
and boundary walls,

Built of the ubiquitous stone, culled from the fields, or axed and levered
out of outcrops, sometimes faced or split, sometimes filled with
scrabbled flinders, fitted, mortarless, tight as puzzle pieces,

Built with what would now be torturous lifting, hugging, and lugging,
done under the long, low sun over decades, decades of decades,
the stones settling in subtly, row on row,

Adamant and indistinct as the years themselves, by hard men faceless and
various as the stones themselves.

According to lore, the discontented among them come back at night
during autumn to fields pitch dark beneath the vast broadcast of
stars

To monitor their work, to make repairs to those boundaries that are their
bonds with this world.

Each has many, many headstones, none with a name.

They did not (O, onanistic onomastician!) make names for themselves,
those men,

But wallstones, and courses of them, since stone by stone makes a wall,
and walls make farming, and farming, homes.

Homes they went back to at dusk and maybe beat their women in, in the
unbeatable heat, and maybe had hard or fearful sex in, as the
parching *meltémi* lashed the night and the fishermen's lashed-up
boats apart,

And anyway yelled things they sometimes did not think could be set down
    in words,

Who set these stones they harvested in place for all but ever.

4

I come because, above the oldest bases of the walls, hunks of strata large
    enough one sees why Titans needed to be conjured,

A former Roman Catholic church contains in three small rooms remains of
    a treasury, which is a *thisavrós,* which is a *thesaurus,* which is also
    why I come,

And a marble fragment one could hold in one hand like a bunch of grapes,
    itself a treasure, a clutch of breasts from a copy of the Ephesian
    goddess (herself a copy of a wooden effigy decked with strings of
    tear-shaped amber beads),

And several "parting scenes," the people in chitons and himations, from
    funerary sculptures.

I come to find these smaller puzzles and pieces of puzzles and to find the
    small peace that lies in that.

To find the only bougainvillea I have ever seen that has been trimmed and
    pleached to look like a tree, until you get up close and see that it
    entwines itself like time itself in a kind of solo orgy,

And then remind yourself of what he wrote, that *truth* shoots out from the
    same root as *tree* not because it is steadfast but because it keeps
    branching and can be pruned.

To sip each evening's ouzo, which is truly mother's milk when ice is
    added (as he, smiling, would understand).

To loaf and invite the soul and discover anew rabbit stew and be
    ridiculously pleased that it is an item in a *katálogos,*

And once a week religiously to gorge on goat and retsina (ah, *efcharistó* is
    exactly what we must say, he could have said), so tough on the
    hillside in the crucifying sun and so forgivingly tender after three
    days in the pot.

I come because from its peak this island with its bights and spits is a
    puzzle piece among others in the archipelago, mountains up to
    their necks in blue-green solitude.

5

I come back here to rough it, to rough it out, to draft, to draw. To
    withdraw—and to *vise* my self, as they once said, and to revise, or
    let it stand and deliver. Make it stand and confess. Out of chagrin.
    And in embarrassment. Out of shame. And in humiliation.

I come back here with my notebook and the amber kombolöi he gave me
    like a least rosary of 33 beads to tell, to say *min ksechnáte,*
    carefully, over and over, alone on a path outside one of the 365
    "churches" the guide book assures me—without elucidation—are
    here, because at home, indelibly and in public, I forgot how to say
    don't forget.

To remember for instance that while our word *fast* runs from and to itself,
    and the word pronounced *akrivós* cleaves instantly, *permanent* and
    quick overlap like small waves, as do *expensive* and *exactly,* and
    anyway they are all one word if we could spell.

To find not that word but sherds of it here and there, as in *petrochórto,* or
    stonecrop, ancient remedy and poison. *Stonecrop.*

(And then to recall that *kápou-kápou* means at once *now and then* and
    here and there and feel for a moment I might be getting warmer.)

To walk out in search of a shaft of the fabulous and flooded mines and
    come across a sarcophagus that is the goats' water trough.

To pick one fieldstone up and bang it with a larger one into a chink in the
    terrace wall beneath the *kastro,* from which one can see the other
    islands' eidolons afloat in the *in-between*—ultramarine—
    ultramundane—Plato's *tó metaxí*—anyone's and no one's,

And where someone, no one now, built long ago flush into the wall where
    the steep path turns firmly as a verse enjambed an ancient basin—
    unobtrusive as a fit quote—its marble weathering to rock again,
    and someone installed above it a modern spigot. And then
    removed the handle.

6

I come back to learn the Greek for *handle.*

To find by the way the Scrabble trove *paremia* meant first a thing
    discovered either "by the route" or "by the song," something used
    and left by those who went before.

To saunter for a jaunty moment along the quay, to wonder at the water,
    to see that the sea's ceaselessness makes the proto-watercolor, the
    Idea of watercolor.

To think that while naming shades—of lipstick, say—might be a
    gratifying occupation, and perhaps profession, that is another
    matter entirely—and even possible.

To confirm that each year more fish slip away and leave their shed tints
    wriggling in the shoals like hints of souls.

To discover that nothing changes. Or only nothing does. Changes
    everything. Always has done, will do. Will have to do, here at the
    end of the day.

It soughs, it saws softly in the surrounding, redundant *hush,* blue as blue,
    blue of the first water, yet clear in the palms' overflowing cup as
    tsípouro. (*Tsípouro:* a spirit condensed from residue, from *must.*)

I come back thinking to come upon something he might like, moving but dry, moving, yet cold and still, like these shallows, profoundly transparent,

And I am in over my head again, where it all flows, beginning with the simplest language, where once some tongue-slip led to *slime* then slid along to *loam* and *lime* and then *oblivion,*

While even stone is hardly faster, sea creatures secreting shells whose limestone pressed to marble harbors streaming linen.

I come back because I cannot stay away. Because I cannot stay.

I come back to leave. Not to leave a mark, either. To take it, rather. Like a vow. A vow of silence, say.

Or just a *volta,* the evening turn along the littoral that turns imaginal beneath my feet. To take it and to leave it, then. To leave my take—as pirates and directors have it—and to take my leave.

from *The Yale Review*

CONTRIBUTORS' NOTES AND COMMENTS

ELIZABETH ALEXANDER was born in New York City in 1962 and was raised in Washington, DC. She has degrees from Yale University and Boston University and completed her PhD in English at the University of Pennsylvania. She is the author of five books of poems, including *American Sublime* (Graywolf, 2005), and two books of essays and interviews, most recently *Power and Possibility* (University of Michigan Press, 2007). She composed and delivered "Praise Song for the Day" for the inauguration of President Barack Obama on January 20, 2009. The poem was published as a small book from Graywolf Press. Her latest publication is *Crave Radiance: New and Selected Poems, 1990–2010.* Her other collections of poems are *The Venus Hottentot, Body of Life, Antebellum Dream Book, American Sublime,* which was one of three finalists for the Pulitzer Prize, and her first young adult collection (collaboratively written with Marilyn Nelson), *Miss Crandall's School for Young Ladies & Little Misses of Color.* Alexander is the first recipient of the Alphonse Fletcher, Sr. Fellowship for work that "contributes to improving race relations in American society and furthers the broad social goals of the U.S. Supreme Court's Brown v. Board of Education decision of 1954." She is the Thomas E. Donnelley Professor of African American Studies at Yale University and chair of Yale's Department of African American Studies.

Of "Rally," Alexander writes: "There was a beautiful moment in the Obama presidential campaign in late October 2008 when all that could be done had been done. Much that had seemed impossible had transpired. Millions of people had put their muscle and money and shoe leather and hearts and souls into the campaign and all the hope and progress it represented. And so it seemed to me that ardent campaign supporters settled into the mode of saying, let's see what history brings, because we have done everything we can.

"And of course, we did not know what, exactly, the election and then the Obama presidency would bring. History and progress are best

understood in terms of process, not just in big flashy moments. Nothing is instantly reparable. Obama is not a god. Communities are never *not* faced with hard work and struggle. So we struggle on, big we's and little we's. That's where the poem comes from."

SHERMAN ALEXIE was born in 1966 and grew up on the Spokane Indian Reservation. His most recent books are the poetry collection *Face,* from Hanging Loose Press, and *War Dances,* stories and poems from Grove Press. He is lucky enough to be a full-time writer and lives with his family in Seattle.

Alexie writes: " 'Valediction' was inspired by the death of somebody I'd met a few times. He was an amazingly talented man with serious demons. I've struggled with my demons as well, though certainly not as seriously as the subject of this poem, so I suppose I wrote this poem to myself, or to that other self who can feel so hopeless and helpless. And since suicide is so prevalent in the Native American community, and I have a lot of Native readers, I thought this poem might serve a social purpose. On a technical note, I've been writing more formally over the last few years. I work in rhyme and syllabics, and I've found, in the hunt for the right word, by sound or count, that I am often surprised by what happens. It's a good thing: to be surprised by one's poetry. I've been writing poems for twenty-four years, so I've picked up plenty of bad habits. I think the rhymes and syllabics help me escape myself."

RAE ARMANTROUT was born in Vallejo, California, in 1947. She teaches writing at UC San Diego. "Soft Money" is from her collection *Money Shot,* published in 2011 by Wesleyan University Press. Her previous book, *Versed,* also from Wesleyan, won the 2010 Pulitzer Prize.

Armantrout writes: "I started 'Soft Money' after hearing an old Duran Duran song, called either 'Rio' or 'Rio Dancer,' on the radio. Some of the verses I could make out were, 'Rio, Rio dancer 'cross the Rio Grande,' and 'She don't need to understand.' The poem spins out of that standard depiction of an exoticized erotic object. It proceeds to run some changes on the always complex relationship between sex and power."

JOHN ASHBERY was born in Rochester, New York, in 1927. His *Notes from the Air: Selected Later Poems* (Ecco, 2007) won the 2008 Griffin International Prize for Poetry. *The Landscapist,* his collected translations of the poetry of Pierre Martory, was published in 2008 by Sheep

Meadow Press in the United States and by Carcanet in the United Kingdom. The Library of America published the first volume of his *Collected Poems* in fall 2008; his most recent collections are *Planisphere* (Ecco, 2009) and a new translation of Arthur Rimbaud's *Illuminations* (W. W. Norton & Co., 2011). In 2006, the City Council of New York declared April 7 to be John Ashbery Day in perpetuity in New York City. He was the guest editor of *The Best American Poetry 1988*.

JULIANNA BAGGOTT was born in Wilmington, Delaware, in 1969. A poet, novelist, and essayist, she teaches in Florida State University's creative writing program. Her seventeen books include three collections of poetry—most notably *Lizzie Borden in Love* (Southern Illinois University Press, 2006)—and novels under her own name as well as under the pen names N. E. Bode and Bridget Asher. Her recent novels include *The Provence Cure for the Brokenhearted* (Random House, 2010, under Asher) and *Pure* (Grand Central, forthcoming 2012), the first in a dystopic trilogy. Her essays have appeared in *The New York Times, The Washington Post, The Boston Globe,* and NPR.org.

Of "To My Lover, Concerning the Yird-Swine," Baggott writes: "I wrote this series of poems during the lead-up to the 2008 election. I was terrified that the McCain-Palin ticket would win, and I was bereft of language. In fact, I felt abandoned by words and so I sought them out—but not just any words. I sought out abandoned words so that I would have a kinship with them at least. The words that you might not recognize in this poem are not ones I invented. They were all once part of the English language. The first drafts of these poems were incredibly violent and convoluted. I've been swapping poems with fellow poet Frank Giampietro (author of *Begin Anywhere*) for over a decade now. He told me that the poems made no sense, but to keep writing them. And so I did until I finished; then I let them sit.

"(Side note: I was writing a novel during this time called *The Ever Breath* [Random House, 2009], a weird, twisted novel for kids aged nine to thirteen or so. I'd fallen in love with the abandoned words and started using them to create this other world. My genres tend to blur. The poems inform the novels—not as often the other way around.)

"When I returned to the poems six months later, I worked as their translator. I refocused them so that they would make sense. I introduced 'my lover,' and with that new purpose, the poems found some order, and eventually, two of the poems found a home at *AGNI* and now here.

"And so, oddly enough, this is how the words themselves have clawed their way back into our mouths."

ERIN BELIEU was born in Omaha, Nebraska, in 1967. She is the author of three poetry collections, *Infanta, One Above & One Below,* and *Black Box,* all from Copper Canyon Press. *Black Box* was a finalist for the *Los Angeles Times* Book Prize. She is the director of the creative writing program at Florida State University and is cofounder, with Cate Marvin, of Vida: Women in Literary Arts.

Belieu writes: " 'When at a Certain Party in NYC' was written shortly after attending a sequence of posh, arty events I had somehow been invited to. I think of it as a kind of blurt of humorous self-loathing mixed with a class warrior's point of view. As is true of many of my poems, I think it engages with that feeling of having come from one world and then finding one's self in another that is both seductive and strangely repellent. Personally, I never want to be too exquisite to live. Oh, and it's dedicated to Mark Bibbins, who does not, in fact, have a Lacanian dildo for a soap dispenser."

CARA BENSON was born in Huntington, New York, in 1967. She is the author of two books of poetry: *(made)* (BookThug, 2010) and *Protean Parade* (Black Radish Books, 2011). She is an active committee member of the PEN Prison Writing Program and teaches poetry in a New York state prison. Her chapbook *Quantum Chaos and Poems: A Manifest(o)ation* won the bpNichol Chapbook Award. Benson is the editor of the interdisciplinary book *Predictions* (ChainLinks, 2009). Her online home is www.necessetics.com.

Of "Banking," Benson writes: "I wrote this poem during the 2008 presidential election season."

JASWINDER BOLINA was born in Chicago, Illinois, in 1978. He is the author of *Carrier Wave* (Center for Literary Publishing, Colorado State University, 2007), winner of the 2006 Colorado Prize for Poetry. He teaches at Columbia College Chicago, where he was the 2010–11 Liberal Arts and Sciences Emerging Poet-in-Residence.

Of "Mine Is the First Rodeo, Mine Is the Last Accolade," Bolina writes, "The poem began with the idea of a birthmark in the shape of Martin van Buren. This image somehow led to a meditation on aftermath, both personal and national, and a speaker who deals with his feelings of nostalgia and resignation with a measure of wryness. This

seems to be his best recourse in the wake of catastrophe, and I can't tell whether it makes him bitter or wise."

CATHERINE BOWMAN was born in El Paso, Texas, in 1957. She is the author of four books of poems: *The Plath Cabinet* (Four Way Books, 2009), *Notarikon* (Four Way Books, 2006), *Rock Farm* (Gibbs Smith, 1996), and *1-800-HOT-RIBS* (Gibbs Smith, 1993). Carnegie Mellon Press reprinted *1-800-HOT-RIBS* in 2000. She is the editor of *Word of Mouth, Poems Featured on NPR's* All Things Considered (Vintage, 2003), an anthology of the poems that she presented on NPR from 1995 to 2002. She teaches in the MFA Creative Writing Program at Indiana University. She lives on a farm in Bloomington, Indiana.

Bowman writes: "I started writing 'The Sink' with this material: a memory of a long-lost friend who told me he liked to talk on the phone while washing the dinner dishes, the many and often contradictory meanings of the word *sink,* the coffee can of bacon fat that lived underneath the kitchen sink when I was a child, a smattering of words associated with war and battle that I wanted to weave in with everyday diction and some strange and not often used words starting with *l* to, perhaps, imitate the L-shaped pipes leading down to the underworld. This poem might be informed by Paul Muldoon's poem 'The Briefcase.'"

TURNER CASSITY was born in 1929 in Jackson, Mississippi, and died in 2009 in Decatur, Georgia. His grandparents on both the maternal and paternal sides were in the sawmill business. His mother, a violinist, and his grandmother, a pianist, were silent-movie musicians. Cassity's father died when he was four, and at the age of sixteen he began managing his own inheritance. In 1951 he graduated from Millsaps College in Jackson, and then enrolled at Stanford University, earning a master's degree in English in 1952. After military service in the Korean War, he attended Columbia University on the GI Bill and received a master's degree in library science in 1955. He worked for the Jackson Public Library and then moved to South Africa, where he worked from 1958 to 1960 as a librarian, first in Pretoria and then near Johannesburg. In 1962 Cassity accepted the position of librarian in the Robert W. Woodruff Library at Emory University in Atlanta, from which he retired in 1991. His ten collections of poetry include *The Destructive Element: New and Selected Poems* (Ohio University Press, 1998), *No Second Eden* (Swallow Press, 2002), and *Devils & Islands* (Swallow Press, 2007). He was awarded a National Endowment for the Arts fellowship, the Michael Braude Award of

the American Academy of Arts and Letters, and the Ingram Merrill Foundation Award. In one of the poems in *No Second Eden,* he adopts the persona of J. P. Morgan: "All you who view me with alarm, / You are the weak who do the harm. / Markets are chaos, structures banks. / Exchanges panic, break their ranks. / I flog them back. I get no thanks."

MICHAEL CIRELLI was born in Providence, Rhode Island, in 1975. His newest collection, *Everyone Loves the Situation* (Penmanship Books, 2011) deconstructs MTV's hit reality show *Jersey Shore,* flipping the cultural zeitgeist on its (gelled and sprayed) head. He is also the author of *Vacations on the Black Star Line* (Hanging Loose Press, 2010), which was named in About.com's Poetry Picks "Best Books of 2010," and *Lobster with Ol' Dirty Bastard* (Hanging Loose Press, 2008). He is the executive director of one of the nation's largest youth literary arts organizations, Urban Word NYC, and has written two poetry curricula, *Poetry Jam* (Recorded Books, 2010) and *Hip-Hop Poetry & the Classics* (Milk Mug, 2004). He has appeared on HBO's *Def Poetry Jam* and *Brave New Voices.*

Cirelli writes: " 'Dead Ass' epitomizes much of what has driven my writing for the past eight years. As the director of a nonprofit organization that serves over twenty-five thousand New York City teen poets each year, I am surrounded by innovative, evolving, fresh, and startling language every day. It is young people who are driving the language machine through hip-hop, through culture, through the multiple linguistics they use to navigate the multiple worlds they inhabit. These teens are bursting open how we communicate and accelerating the velocity with which we communicate (through texting, Twitter, Facebook) and sometimes it's hard for me to keep up, being older and 'alabaster.' The poem addresses my compulsion for these new poetics but also addresses some of the race dynamics that are caught up in it. My career has been dedicated to championing these young voices, and articulating the value and importance of hip-hop culture, as well as the poetic form of 'rap.' This poem was attached to an essay that was my MFA thesis at the New School. Published almost in full, the essay, originally titled 'Blasting the Canon: Hip-Hop Poetics, Race & the Ivory Tower,' became part of *The New York Quarterly*'s 'The Present State of American Poetry' series, under the subtitle 'Hip-Hop.'

"Eventually, my first and second collections of poems, *Lobster with Ol' Dirty Bastard,* where 'Dead Ass' also appeared, and *Vacations on the Black Star Line,* not only tried to pull up a seat for hip-hop culture at the academy's table, but also looked at the racial consequences of my

doing it, with one foot in both worlds. The poems were sonnets, odes, and word portraits dedicated to the iconography of hip-hop culture, and the audience they were intended for was as wide as my blurbers, from David Lehman to Kanye West. 'Dead Ass' seems to encapsulate all that I love about this work, while also exposing my vulnerability in its execution."

BILLY COLLINS was born in the French Hospital in New York City in 1941. He was an undergraduate at Holy Cross College and received his PhD from the University of California, Riverside. His books of poetry include *Horoscopes for the Dead* (Random House, 2011), *Ballistics* (Random House, 2008), *The Trouble with Poetry and Other Poems* (Random House, 2005), a collection of haiku titled *She Was Just Seventeen* (Modern Haiku Press, 2006), *Nine Horses* (Random House, 2002), *Sailing Alone Around the Room: New and Selected Poems* (Random House, 2001), *Picnic, Lightning* (University of Pittsburgh Press, 1998), *The Art of Drowning* (University of Pittsburgh Press, 1995), and *Questions About Angels* (William Morrow, 1991), which was selected for the National Poetry Series by Edward Hirsch and reprinted by the University of Pittsburgh Press in 1999. He is the editor of *Poetry 180: A Turning Back to Poetry* (Random House, 2003) and *180 More: Extraordinary Poems for Every Day* (Random House, 2005). He is a Distinguished Professor of English at Lehman College (City University of New York) and a Distinguished Fellow of the Winter Park Institute of Rollins College. A frequent contributor and former guest editor of *The Best American Poetry* series, he was appointed United States Poet Laureate 2001–2003 and served as New York State Poet 2004–2006. He also edited *Bright Wings: An Anthology of Poems about Birds,* illustrated by David Sibley (Columbia University Press, 2010).

Collins writes: " 'Here and There' does not encourage literary glibness in me, so I will say only what should be obvious: that the poem follows the avoidance strategies of a mind unable to deal directly with a very grave matter. Daunted by the reality of his friend's crisis, the speaker seeks refuge in his habit of writing about imaginary things; but we see that this carries a price as his actual memories and the present scene around him become imbued with a similar unreality. The poem ends with a wishful gesture as the speaker, stuck in denial, tries to protect himself and the friend by placing her dire predicament in the realm of the fantastic. Inside the easy cliché of the title is the fact of his distance from the friend, who is truly in another place."

OLENA KALYTIAK DAVIS was born in 1963 in Detroit, Michigan. Ukrainian was her first language. She has published three books of poetry: *And Her Soul Out of Nothing* (University of Wisconsin Press, 1997); *shattered sonnets love cards and other off and back handed importunities* (Bloomsbury/Tin House, 2003), and *On the Kitchen Table from Which Everything Has Been Hastily Removed* (Hollyridge, 2009); and her work has appeared in four earlier volumes of *The Best American Poetry* (1995, 2000, 2001, 2004), sometimes under *D* for Davis and sometimes under *K* for Kalytiak. She lives in Anchorage, Alaska, where she buoyantly raises her two children and writes appellate briefs to pay the mortgage.

Of her sonnets Davis writes: "These are from my how-quickly-can-you-turn-life-into-art phase of false love and ecstasy-induced enthusiasm in the late summer, early fall of 2009. Turns out, pretty quickly; and, unfortunately, that's almost the same rate at which the mania passes."

MATTHEW DICKMAN was born in Portland, Oregon, in 1975, and was raised there. He is a member of the poetry faculty at the Vermont College of Fine Arts low-residency MFA program. The author of *All-American Poem* (*The American Poetry Review* Prize, 2008), he is the recipient of a Honickman First Book Prize, the May Sarton Award from the American Academy of Arts and Sciences, the Kate Tufts Award from Claremont College, and the 2009 Oregon Book Award. His second book, *Mayakovsky's Revolver,* is forthcoming from W. W. Norton & Co. He lives in Portland, Oregon.

Dickman writes: "All of my poems begin in a very simple place. Usually a meditation on something I like or am afraid of. From this 'diving board' the mind can go anywhere. This is how 'Coffee' happened. I was thinking about how much I liked Portland coffee such as Stumptown, Water Ave, and Cellar Door. This meditation drew me toward the death of my older brother. Somehow, in a meaningful way for me, the two intimate subjects balanced each other and allowed me to think about each in a more complicated way than if I had thought of them separately. I love coffee. I miss my older brother. Poetry is often the 'meaning-making creature' through which we understand our lives."

MICHAEL DICKMAN was born in Portland, Oregon, in 1975, and was raised there. He is the author of two books of poems, *The End of the West* (2009) and *Flies* (2011), both published by Copper Canyon Press.

Of "From the Lives of My Friends," Dickman writes: "I read someplace that Anton Chekhov had wanted to write a novel called *Stories*

from the Lives of My Friends, but didn't. What a great title, I remember thinking. Another thing about Dr. Chekhov that I read was that when he died and his body was shipped to Moscow, he was packed in ice in a refrigerated car marked 'Oysters' on the outside. Some way to go."

DENISE DUHAMEL was born in Providence, Rhode Island, in 1961. Her most recent books are *Ka-Ching!* (University of Pittsburgh Press, 2009), *Two and Two* (Pittsburgh, 2005), *Mille et un Sentiments* (Firewheel, 2005), *Queen for a Day: Selected and New Poems* (Pittsburgh, 2001), *The Star-Spangled Banner* (Southern Illinois University Press, 1999), and *Kinky* (Orchises Press, 1997). A bilingual edition of her poems, *Afortunada de mí (Lucky Me),* translated into Spanish by Dagmar Buchholz and David González, came out in 2008 with Bartleby Editores (Madrid). She is a professor of English at Florida International University in Miami.

Duhamel writes: "The poem 'My Strip Club' began in response to a Pole Dance Doll that may have been issued in 2008 by an Asian toy company to sell to off-price retailers. This doll was not a novelty item for adults meant to titillate—it was actually a child's toy. A traditional-looking doll was packaged with a blinking stripper pole and disco ball as accessories. There was such an outcry in the blogosphere about the Pole Dance Doll's inappropriateness that I didn't have much to add. Some writers pondered—and hoped—that the toy was a Photoshopped hoax. Still, a similar toy, a Peekaboo Pole Dancing Kit, was pulled from Tesco shelves in Britain in 2006. I began to think about the extent to which nude and semi-nude female bodies are commonplace in our present-day culture and wondered if, at some point, concealing—rather than revealing—will awaken sexual desire. I don't think that will ever be the case, of course, but I was intrigued to write a poem in which dressing was just as erotic as undressing."

Born in 1954, CORNELIUS EADY was raised in Rochester, New York. He is the author of *Hardheaded Weather* (G. P. Putnam's Sons, 2008); *Brutal Imagination* (G. P. Putnam's Sons, 2001), which was a finalist for the 2001 National Book Award in poetry; *the autobiography of a jukebox* (Carnegie Mellon University Press 1997); *You Don't Miss Your Water* (Henry Holt and Company, 1995); *The Gathering of My Name* (Carnegie Mellon, 1991); *BOOM BOOM BOOM* (State Street Press, 1988); *Victims of the Latest Dance Craze* (Ommation Press, 1985); and *Kartunes* (Warthog Press, 1980). In 1996, Eady and the poet Toi Derricotte founded Cave Canem, a nonprofit organization serving black poets of various backgrounds and

providing a space for intellectual engagement and critical debate. Along with Derricotte, he also edited *Gathering Ground* (University of Michigan Press, 2006). He has collaborated with jazz composer Deidre Murray in the production of several works of musical theater, including *You Don't Miss Your Water* and *Running Man*. He has won the *Prairie Schooner* Strousse Award, a Lila Wallace–Reader's Digest Writer's Award, and fellowships from the Guggenheim Foundation, the National Endowment for the Arts, and the Rockefeller Foundation. He lives in Columbia, Missouri, where he holds the Miller Chair in Poetry at University of Missouri.

JILL ALEXANDER ESSBAUM was born in Bay City, Texas, in 1971. Her most recent books include *Harlot* (No Tell Books, 2007) and a single-poem chapbook, *The Devastation* (Cooper Dillon Books, 2009). She teaches in the University of California, Riverside–Palm Desert Low Residency MFA program.

Of "Stays," Essbaum writes: "I can recall with absolute clarity the day I wrote this poem. My (now) ex-husband had come home for lunch. We lived in a small town outside of Zürich, Switzerland. We had been fighting and discussing (with as much aplomb and grace as we could find in ourselves) a divorce. In fact, we had decided on a divorce. On the day I wrote this poem, I was possessed by both a terrible despair and a wrenching anger. They were knocking upon the door of my heart. Loudly. With undeniable fists. There was nothing I could do but write.

"When Axel came home for lunch, he took me to our favorite of the town's two restaurants. I ate a pizza. It was spicy. Axel had the salmon he never failed to order. And as we waited for the waiter to bring our food, I read him this poem (then, it was my custom to read him all my poems, even ones such as this). Axel said he thought it was really good but it made him sad. 'Well, *yeah* . . . ' I remember responding. His favorite lines? 'I reach / For the one-two punch of panic pills. / You sit and sort the bills. *A pair of parallel hells.*'

"All of this I mention because . . . well, because he doesn't come off too well in this poem. And because our marriage wasn't all bad all the time. And because I no longer hate him. And because he was extremely supportive of the poems I wrote, even when he was the central character. And because that's a pretty damn difficult thing to do. And because I'm glad he was like that.

"And even though I stand by the circumstances of this poem, I need to make clear something that the poem simply doesn't address: *Once, and for many years, we loved each other.*"

ALAN FELDMAN was born in New York City in 1945 and was raised in Woodmere, on the south shore of Long Island. He entered Columbia College in 1962 and took Kenneth Koch's first-year writing class as well as his humanities survey. Already a fan of the New York poets, particularly Frank O'Hara, he wrote a paper for Koch that eventually became a PhD dissertation at SUNY Buffalo and was published as *Frank O'Hara* (1979) in Twayne's United States Authors Series. Columbia Review Press published his first book of poems, *The Household* (1966). His second collection, *The Happy Genius* (Sun, 1978), won the annual George Elliston Book Award for the best collection published by a small, independent press in the United States. *The Personals,* a chapbook, came out in 1982, and *Anniversary,* self-published, with drawings by his wife, Nan Hass Feldman, in 1992. They also collaborated on *Round Trip* (2003), *On the Zocalo* (2007), and *The Blue Boat* (2010), all chapbooks with artwork. *A Sail to Great Island* (2004), his most recent full-length collection, won the Pollak Prize for Poetry at the University of Wisconsin. Feldman is former chair of the English department and professor emeritus at Framingham (MA) State University, where he taught for thirty-seven years. For more than two decades he also taught the advanced creative writing class at the Radcliffe Seminars, Harvard University. He spends his summers in Wellfleet on Cape Cod, where, for the past several years, he and Tony Hoagland have been offering a free drop-in workshop every week at the public library.

Of "In November," Feldman writes: "I've come to like this kind of teaching so much that I started a similar workshop during the school year at the library in Framingham. Since I don't get paid, and the students don't get any credit, they don't have to please me and I don't have to lie, as the protagonist of Nicholson Baker's *Anthologist* complains, to make a living. The format is always the same. Before looking at their manuscripts, we start with an 'in-class' writing prompt or assignment. People read what they come up with (optional).

"The assignment that day was to write a poem that was all one long sentence. (I wanted them to practice using stretched-out syntax.) We'd first read over some examples: 'Danse Russe' by William Carlos Williams; 'I Wish I Knew a Woman' by D. H. Lawrence; 'Greed and Aggression' by Sharon Olds; 'Apology (To the Muse)' by Alan Dugan; 'Notoriety' by W. B. Yeats; and Shakespeare's 'When in disgrace with fortune and men's eyes.' (Admittedly, to make all of these one-sentence poems, you sometimes have to change the punctuation a bit, as I later did, in reverse, with my poem, adding a few full stops, but changing

little else.) I'd been thinking all day about my daughter's impromptu visit. They were writing and I was writing (we usually spend about twenty minutes) and suddenly the tree came along (visiting from Yeats's 'Prayer for My Daughter'—only in Yeats the daughter is the tree!) and that unpredictability made me think it would be fun to read to them what I'd written. I don't often. But the story came across very clearly to them, I think, and I was pleased when Emily Wheeler, one of the students, pronounced, 'That's a keeper.'"

FARRAH FIELD was born in Cheyenne, Wyoming, in 1976, and now lives in Brooklyn, where she is co-host of an event series called Yardmeter Editions. She is the author of *Rising* (Four Way Books, 2009) and the chapbook *Parents* (Immaculate Disciples Press, 2011). Her second book of poetry will appear from Four Way Books in 2012. She occasionally blogs at adultish.blogspot.com and is co-owner of Berl's Brooklyn Poetry Shop.

Field writes: "The Amy poems came about when I was working on an untitled cluster of poems focusing on various women I know. I wanted the poems to be joined by one name, a feminine one, a sort of youthful one. Around the same time I was looking for cover art for my first book, and upon my suggestion, my editors asked a Brooklyn artist named Amy if we could use one of her paintings. Amy or her representatives said no. Feeling rejected and angry, I have included the name Amy in all the titles of the poems I've been working on since then.

"The initial red force of the Amy poems as seen in 'You're Really Starting to Suck, Amy' exemplifies the Marx Brothers–type anger, the say-no-to-*this!* rebuffs that pepper the poems. This is not to say there isn't exploration of the body and art, feelings of being snubbed and lost, and vengeful counter-rejection rejection; however, the Amy poems, at least for me, investigate the broad and complicated question as to why women, and everyone else really, are taught to take women apart as though no one could possibly appreciate or understand a woman unless she was broken and flawed. The aimlessness apparent in 'Amy Survives Another Apocalypse' focuses on how even the last woman standing can't do anything because she is so afraid of doing the wrong thing and furthermore has no one there to tell her what to do. So you can view painter Amy's wonderful work on the cover of Lorrie Moore's *A Gate at the Stairs* while with these two particular Amy poems, you can see how poetic investigation transforms discontent into understanding and celebration."

CAROLYN FORCHÉ was born in Detroit, Michigan, in 1950. She is the author of four books of poetry, most recently *Blue Hour* (HarperCollins, 2003), and editor of *Against Forgetting: Twentieth-Century Poetry of Witness* (W. W. Norton & Co.). She is professor of English at Georgetown University, where she directs the Lannan Center for Poetics and Social Practice.

Forché indicates that "Morning on the Island" was "written on an island in the Pacific Northwest, and has something to do with the ravages of global warming on flora and fauna, with invasive species and species endangerment, pernicious tourism, and the beauty of appearances. The last line touches upon species extinction. It is also a brief lyric poem evoking a place with, I hope, some tenderness."

BECKIAN FRITZ GOLDBERG was born in Hartford, Wisconsin, in 1954, but grew up in Arizona. She holds an MFA from Vermont College and is the author of several volumes of poetry: *Body Betrayer* (Cleveland State University Press, 1991); *In the Badlands of Desire* (Cleveland State University Press, 1993); *Never Be the Horse*, winner of the University of Akron Poetry Prize (University of Akron Press, 1999); *Twentieth Century Children*, a limited-edition chapbook (Graphic Design Press, Indiana University, 1999); *Lie Awake Lake*, winner of the 2004 Field Poetry Prize (Oberlin College Press, 2005); *The Book of Accident* (University of Akron Press, 2006); and *Reliquary Fever: New and Selected Poems* (New Issues Press, 2010). She is professor of English in the creative writing program at Arizona State University.

Of "Everything Is Nervous," Goldberg writes: "I don't know where the blue flowers came from. They are a hallucination as far as I know. The bullets in the poem are real. I'm pretty sure the murder victim was named Vince. It's not unusual to find me watching *Forensic Files* or *Cold Case Files,* or any number of similar shows, late at night. It's not unusual to find me writing with the TV on at a low drone. If I turn from my desk and look left, I can glance at the picture. Those were the circumstances that led to this poem. The murder case I was listening to took place in Little Rock and that's how Little Rock took its place in the poem. I'm pretty sure the cop stole his dialogue from the cop in the show. Thievery and murder find their way into the poem after the unsolvable blue. I remember writing the first draft in one sitting. I'd been surprised by the ending but it stuck. Then I had a cigarette on the patio. It was late October and the nights were almost bearable, meaning the five straight months of searing heat were finally over, and

the change, the feeling of the world—the nonhuman world—being on the edge of something, or between, the feeling of another time right up against you: all this, I think, had been a catalyst for the poem."

BENJAMIN S. GROSSBERG was born in New York City in 1971. He is the author of two full-length poetry collections: *Sweet Core Orchard* (University of Tampa Press, 2009), winner of the Tampa Review Prize and a Lambda Literary Award, and *Underwater Lengths in a Single Breath* (Ashland Poetry Press, 2007), which won the Snyder Prize. A chapbook, *The Auctioneer Bangs His Gavel,* was published by Kent State University Press in 2006. He teaches creative writing at the University of Hartford and serves as an assistant poetry editor and book reviewer for *Antioch Review.* His third full-length collection, *Space Traveler,* will be published by the University of Tampa Press in 2013.

Grossberg writes: "With the Space Traveler series, my mask has never felt thinner. Sometimes I think these poems aren't so much dramatic monologues as lyrics based on an extended metaphor. Or maybe just lyrics written by someone who watched too much *Star Trek* growing up.

"This entry in the series began with something I heard on a radio program, that everything which makes us—all the elements—were created inside of stars. I carried this idea around for a few months before it found a place at the center of this poem, spawning the line of thought that resulted in the final image: a wandering Earth as an emblem for the desiring self. As far out in the Galaxy as the Space Traveler flies, he usually seems to end up back at the landscape of desire."

JENNIFER GROTZ was born in Canyon, Texas, in 1971. Currently she teaches at the University of Rochester and in the low-residency MFA program at Warren Wilson College. She also serves as the assistant director of the Bread Loaf Writers' Conference. Her first book, *Cusp,* was chosen by Yusef Komunyakaa for the 2003 Bakeless Prize. Her second book, *The Needle,* appeared from Houghton Mifflin Harcourt in 2011.

Grotz writes: " 'Poppies' is the first poem I wrote at the Monastère de Saorge, a former Franciscan monastery in the maritime Alps of France. For the past two summers, I've spent month-long retreats there, astonishingly isolated from the world of ATMs and telephones, television, radio, mass transportation, or Internet. After the first couple of days of panic and restlessness, I fell in love with the place: its frescoes, its mountains, its gardens, its poppies, its peacocks, its cherries, its moths."

ROBERT HASS was born in San Francisco in 1941. His books include *Field Guide* (Yale University Press, 1973), *Praise* (Ecco, 1979), *Twentieth Century Pleasures* (Ecco, 1984), *Human Wishes* (Ecco, 1989), *The Essential Haiku: Versions of Bashō, Buson, and Issa* (Ecco, 1994), *Sun Under Wood* (Ecco, 1996), *Now and Then: The Poet's Choice Columns* (Counterpoint, 2007), *Time and Materials* (Ecco, 2007), and *The Apple Trees at Olema* (Ecco, 2010). He has also translated, with the author, a number of volumes of the poetry of Czesław Miłosz, including *Unattainable Earth* (Ecco, 1985), *Provinces* (Ecco, 1991), *Facing the River* (Ecco, 1995), *A Road-side Dog* (Ecco, 1998), *A Treatise on Poetry* (Ecco, 2001), and *Second Space* (Ecco, 2004). He teaches in the English department at the University of California at Berkeley. He was the guest editor of *The Best American Poetry 2001*.

Hass writes: "I wrote the first drafts of the 'August Notebook: A Death' poems on consecutive days after the death of my brother Jim Hass. The title of the first of them comes from a remark in C. D. Wright's *Cooling Time*. 'Sometimes,' she writes, 'a poet just wants to say *river, bicycle, peony*. Judith Moore's essay on the African American morticians of California can be found in *The Left Coast of Paradise* (Soho Press, 1987). Judith Moore is a wonderful and surprising writer who died in the spring of 2006. 'Louis Collins' was recorded on December 21, 1928, in New York City. Mississippi John Hurt said, when asked about this ballad of a small-town shooting, that he 'made it up from hearing people talk. He was killed by two men named Bob and Louis. I got enough of the story to write me a song.'"

TERRANCE HAYES was born in Columbia, South Carolina, in 1971. He won the National Book Award in poetry for *Lighthead*, his most recent poetry collection. His other books are *Wind in a Box*, *Muscular Music*, and *Hip Logic*. He has received a Whiting Writers' Award, a National Endowment for the Arts Fellowship, and a Guggenheim Fellowship. He is a professor of creative writing at Carnegie Mellon University and lives in Pittsburgh, Pennsylvania.

Of "Lighthead's Guide to the Galaxy," Hayes writes: "This poem is a sort of Ars Poetica—or a collection of *ars poetical* flashes . . . Jack French, my late college English professor, was a handsome, old-school hard-ass. He often cussed his unprepared students and kicked them out of class, his office always engulfed in a bluish smoke. He bred horses and bled whiskey. Once in the midst of reading Molly Bloom's soliloquy at the end of *Ulysses* he began suddenly softly weeping before us, a class of knuckle-headed sophomores. I'm glad the poem holds that moment.

Here's the end of that rejoicing Joyce passage: 'and then I asked him with my eyes to ask again yes and then he asked me would I yes to say yes my mountain flower and first I put my arms around him yes and drew him down to me so he could feel my breasts all perfume yes and his heart was going like mad and yes I said yes I will Yes.'"

K. A. HAYS was born in Phoenixville, Pennsylvania, in 1980. She studied English literature and the literary arts at Bucknell, Oxford, and Brown Universities. Hays is the author of two books of poetry, *Dear Apocalypse* (Carnegie Mellon University Press, 2009) and the forthcoming *Early Creatures, Native Gods* (Carnegie Mellon University Press, 2012). She lives in Lewisburg, Pennsylvania, and teaches creative writing at Bucknell.

Of "Just As, After a Point, Job Cried Out," Hayes writes: "As I worked on this and other poems in my second book, I was thinking of spiritual doubt and of the world's indifference to the suffering of its inhabitants. I drafted the poem not long after a flood in my town. We had a warm spell during an otherwise harsh winter, and the ground had not thawed, so when it rained, the rain had nowhere to go. As I pumped out my flooded basement, I imagined the ground as having a voice, and as having suffered too much to leave itself open for more. Once the soil itself can speak and threaten, anything can happen— including the appearance of creatures that ride floating billboards, understand the ground's rebellion, and say they would have done the same. The poem—like so many poems—has at its root, I suppose, a desire for empathy: for one suffering entity to understand another."

BOB HICOK was born in Grand Ledge, Michigan, in 1960. His most recent collection is *Words for Empty and Words for Full* (University of Pittsburgh Press, 2010). *This Clumsy Living* (University of Pittsburgh Press, 2007) won the Bobbitt Prize from the Library of Congress and was published in a German translation by luxbooks in 2011. A finalist for the National Book Critics Circle Award, he is the recipient of a Guggenheim, two NEA Fellowships, and five Pushcart Prizes. He is currently an associate professor at Virginia Tech.

Of "Having Intended to Merely Pick on an Oil Company, the Poem Goes Awry," Hicok writes: "This poem was written before the Gulf oil spill. Had it been written after the oil spill, it would have had dead fish and pelicans in it, though some of the cows in the poem have died since the poem was written. You may have eaten some of the cows who have died. 'Died' is obviously a euphemism, as 'you' is in some sense

a euphemism. While the poem suggests I know things about the fore-skins of seraphim, I do not. In the spirit of full disclosure, I don't know anyone who knows much about the foreskins of seraphim. Most of the people I know are generalists, in that they are generally hungry or sleepy or hoping to be understood as essential to the endeavor. By the way, gas prices are going back up, which means interest in alternative sources of energy will go up, until gas prices go down, when interest in alterna-tive energy will go down. The graph of this cycle should be called the Laugher Curve, for obvious reasons."

Born in New York City in 1953 and a resident of Northern California for over thirty years, JANE HIRSHFIELD is the author of seven books of poetry, including *Come, Thief* (Knopf, 2011), and *After* (NY: Harper-Collins, 2006; UK: Bloodaxe, 2006), a finalist for England's T. S. Eliot Prize in Poetry and named a "best book of 2006" by *The Washington Post,* the *San Francisco Chronicle,* and England's *Financial Times.* Her 2001 book, *Given Sugar, Given Salt* (HarperCollins) was a finalist for the National Book Critics Circle Award. She is also the author of a volume of essays, *Nine Gates: Entering the Mind of Poetry* (HarperCollins, 1997) and three books collecting the poems of women poets from the past. Her work has appeared in five previous editions of *The Best American Poetry.* She has received the Poetry Center Book Award, the California Book Award, and fellowships from the Guggenheim and Rockefeller Foundations, the National Endowment for the Arts, and the Academy of American Poets.

Of "The Cloudy Vase," Hirshfield writes: "One of the balancing acts of the heart is between allegiance to what we are carrying in thought and the mind's affections and allegiance to what is just here, this moment's actual and entirely self-sufficient existence. Let us imagine, then, a story: A woman is far from her beloved, who sends flowers. A vase is found in a cupboard. The flowers are put on the table where she works, to remind her, as intended, of that other life, a life that can be returned to, where love still exists. After a time, the rose petals drop, the irises withdraw and their leaves dull, the delphinium turn introspective. At first, the woman recuts the stems, lifts out the ones that look worst. The last stalks stand in the vase for as long as, and longer than, makes any sense. Finally the whole arrangement is an undeniable wreck, and the flowers, the water with its exuberating algae, are emptied. The woman washes the vase and sets it down on the kitchen counter. What is left then is simple and undomesticable—the curve of empty, clear

glass in the sunlight; the vanishment-tiger clarity that waits past the edge of every story."

PAUL HOOVER was born in Harrisonburg, Virginia, in 1946. He is a professor of creative writing at San Francisco State University. He is editor of the anthology *Postmodern American Poetry* (W. W. Norton & Co., 1994) and coeditor of the literary annual *New American Writing*. His recent poetry volumes are *Sonnet 56* (Les Figues Press, 2009), consisting of fifty-six versions of Shakespeare's sonnet 56; *Edge and Fold* (Apogee Press, 2006); and *Poems in Spanish* (Omnidawn Publishing, 2005). With Maxine Chernoff, he edited and translated *Selected Poems of Friedrich Hölderlin* (Omnidawn Publishing, 2008), which won the PEN-USA Translation Award for 2009. With Nguyen Do, he edited and translated *Beyond the Court Gate: Selected Poems of Nguyen Trai* (Counterpath Press, 2010) and the anthology *Black Dog, Black Night: Contemporary Vietnamese Poetry* (Milkweed Editions, 2008). His essay collection, *Fables of Representation,* was published by the University of Michigan Press in 2004. "God's Promises" is one of three poems that won the Frederick Bock Prize of *Poetry* (June 2010).

" 'God's Promises' is part of a manuscript, 'Gravity's Children,' based on books of the Old Testament. I began the series around 2001 using the process of 'reading through,' which gives a taste or impression of themes and events. I was also testing new forms. For instance, the title poem, based on Esther, consists entirely of a dialogue, complete with stage directions. As I approached Job, I felt the limit of my ability to carry on the sequence and put it into suspension, but years later, in 2009, I started writing again with fresh energy gained from the books of prophecy, of which Zephaniah is one. Instead of reading through, I began to give voice to the prophets' visions and also to allude to disorderly events of our own time."

ANDREW HUDGINS writes that he "was born on the post hospital at Fort Hood, Texas, in 1951. I teach at Ohio State University, along with my wife, the fiction writer Erin McGraw, and our great love has resulted in two adoptions: a labradoodle named Max and a coonhound mix named Sister. Their predecessors, Rosie and Buddy, reside in separate, ash-filled boxes on a bookshelf in the living room. It's hard when you outlive your children, but easier if your children are dogs.

"Although I write in the poem about my father's funeral, he is still alive, though frail, and living alone in Albertville, Alabama—the Fire

Hydrant Capital of the World. He's eighty-eight now, and I've been rehearsing his death for two decades, thinking about it, preparing myself for it—expecting it, dreading it. Last summer, he divvied up some of our inheritance. He placed before us the art we grew up with, and we took turns selecting. Because I chose first, I got the least chipped Hummel, plus three cracked and reglued ones in the later rounds, as well as a carved mahogany elephant that still has one of its real ivory tusks.

"Three years ago my much-loved father-in-law died at eighty-seven, and I found myself projecting his California, Catholic funeral onto what I imagine my father's Southern Baptist funeral will be like in Alabama. A couple of months ago, I looked up the actuarial charts, and since Dad lives a clean life, he might make it to ninety-two. My life expectancy falls short of that."

MAJOR JACKSON is the author of two collections of poetry: *Hoops* (W. W. Norton & Co., 2006) and *Leaving Saturn* (University of Georgia Press, 2002), winner of the Cave Canem Poetry Prize and finalist for a National Book Critics Circle Award. *Holding Company,* his third volume of poetry, is forthcoming from W. W. Norton. He is a recipient of a Whiting Writers' Award and has been honored by the Pew Fellowship in the Arts and the Witter Bynner Foundation in conjunction with the Library of Congress. He served as a creative arts fellow at the Radcliffe Institute for Advanced Study at Harvard University and as the Jack Kerouac Writer-in-Residence at the University of Massachusetts (Lowell). He is the Richard Dennis Green and Gold Professor at the University of Vermont and a core faculty member of the Bennington Writing Seminars. He serves as the poetry editor of the *Harvard Review.*

Jackson writes: "These poems, excerpts of a larger manuscript that would become the book *Holding Company,* were mainly written as exercises in lyric density; in writing them, during a severe moment of personal upheaval, I believed that the brevity of ten crisp lines, driven by associative leaps and dialogical language, would capture the inexhaustible bewilderment and intense feelings of anguish in the midst of a failed relationship and aftermath of illicit loves. I actively resisted narrating in verse my inner suffering and shame, for I felt the details were overly familiar and predictable, yet what could be redemptive is how I represented the truth of my emotional response to personal failure. I understand lyric as the melodic use of language, but I also believe it to be that which is most distinctively expressed, the cry of the self,

hammered out and played in language until it weds itself to the larger story of human struggle and creation. Each poem I write is not only an improvised moment of insinuation and linguistic discovery, but also an utterance that unfolds in the syntactic cathedral that is the poem."

ALLISON JOSEPH was born in 1967 in London, England, to a Jamaican mother and a Grenadian father. Her family moved to Toronto, Canada, when she was four months old, and to the Bronx, New York, when she was four years old. She is a graduate of Kenyon College and Indiana University. She is an associate professor of English at Southern Illinois University in Carbondale, Illinois, where she directs the MFA program in creative writing and helps edit *Crab Orchard Review*, a national journal of creative works. Her most recent poetry collection, *My Father's Kites*, was published in 2010 by Steel Toe Books (Western Kentucky University).

Joseph writes: "I have adored notebooks since I was a very small child. I loved, and still love, their blankness, their efficiency—even their smell. As a poet, I lean toward writing about everyday objects and ordinary things, so what would be better for me to write about than a notebook? Practically all my poems start in notebooks—usually the cheap, drugstore-variety kind—so notebooks represent freedom and fertility to me, that certain volubility and vulnerability I feel when a poem begins to brew within me. When I was a teenager first learning to write poetry, I'd stash my notebooks below my bed, hoping that my parents would not discover what I was doing with words. Now, years later, my notebooks still huddle beneath my bed, beckoning to me to drop everything else and indulge only them. It seemed quite natural that I'd want to sing their praises."

L. S. KLATT was born in Cincinnati, Ohio, in 1962. His first book, *Interloper*, won the 2008 Juniper Prize for Poetry and was published by the University of Massachusetts Press in 2009. His second collection, *Cloud of Ink*, won the 2010 Iowa Poetry Prize and was published by the University of Iowa Press in 2011. He teaches American literature and creative writing at Calvin College in Grand Rapids, Michigan.

Of "Andrew Wyeth, Painter, Dies at 91," Klatt writes: "One of the inspirations for this piece was Andrew Wyeth's painting *Brown Swiss*, which, despite its title, has no cows in it. Wyeth insisted that the cows were indeed there even if not visible. I wanted to reproduce a similar 'presence by absence' in my poem, thinking not only of the Brown

Swiss but of Wyeth himself, who has now disappeared from the earth. I suppose the violence in the poem, and the monstrosity, has something to do with the appropriation of Wyeth for my own artistic purposes. It seems to me that to represent Wyeth—whether in a poem or a biography or an obituary—is necessarily to distort who he really was both in life and on the canvas. The subject is too complex, too elusive. I suppose also that the violence in the poem, besides its shock value, has something to do with curiosity. The giant squid wandered out of my imagination to investigate and then consume the kind of landscape for which Wyeth was famous. But my poem, with its severe and bizarre imagery, is not as iconoclastic as it first appears to be. I am not championing an American surrealism so much as I am expressing how haunted the world is without Andrew Wyeth."

JENNIFER KNOX was born in 1968 in Lancaster, California. Her three books of poems, *The Mystery of the Hidden Driveway* (2010), *Drunk by Noon* (2008), and *A Gringo Like Me* (2005) are available from Bloof Books. She is a graduate of the creative writing program at New York University and has taught poetry writing at Hunter College. This is her fourth appearance in *The Best American Poetry* series. Her work has also appeared in *The New Yorker* and *American Poetry Review*. She lives in Brooklyn, where she is at work on a novel.

Of "Kiri Te Kanawa Singing 'O Mio Babbino Caro,'" Knox writes: "My aunt Marilyn loved Kiri Te Kanawa, but to me, as a teenager, her voice sounded hokey. And not just because it was opera. Twenty years later, her 'O Mio Babbino Caro' came on the radio, and I suddenly found myself sobbing. A theory: when you're a stranger to death, as most kids are, you seek it out—by listening to the Cure, smoking pot in a graveyard, etc. But when you know death, its absence—in a song, a painting, or a poem—is stunning. As an adult, I hear her voice and I cry because I am overwhelmed by death—and even more so by its absence. Or maybe we just get soft and sentimental. Chicken or the egg. Marilyn accepted my sharp edges, but always encouraged me to be a little softer. This poem is for her."

YUSEF KOMUNYAKAA was born in Bogalusa, Louisiana, on April 29, 1947. His several volumes of poetry include *I Apologize for the Eyes in My Head* (1986); *Dien Cai Dau* (1988); *Neon Vernacular: New & Selected Poems 1977–1989* (1993), for which he received the Pulitzer Prize and the Kingsley Tufts Poetry Award; and *Pleasure Dome* (2001), all pub-

lished by Wesleyan University Press; and more recently *Talking Dirty to the Gods* (2000); *Taboo* (2004); and *Warhorses* (2008), all published by Farrar, Straus and Giroux. His recent plays and performance collaborations include *Saturnalia, Wakonda's Dream, Weather Wars,* and *Testimony* (which was performed at the Sydney Opera House). His most recent collection, *The Chameleon Couch,* was published in 2011 by FSG. He currently teaches in the creative writing program at New York University. He was the guest editor of *The Best American Poetry 2003.*

JAMES LONGENBACH was born in Plainfield, New Jersey, in 1959. He is the author of four collections of poems, most recently *The Iron Key* (W. W. Norton & Co., 2010) and *Draft of a Letter* (University of Chicago Press, 2007). He also writes about poetry, and the most recent of his prose books are *The Art of the Poetic Line* (Graywolf, 2008) and *The Resistance to Poetry* (University of Chicago Press, 2004). He teaches at the University of Rochester, where he is the Joseph H. Gilmore Professor of English.

Of "Snow," Longenbach writes: "In the city where I live, it snows a lot, not a little. The citizens are prepared. Therefore, the streets are clear, the schools are rarely closed. One desires so much more than that. 'Neve che cadi dall'alto e noi copri' ('Snow that falls from above and covers us'), wrote the mysteriously plain-spoken Italian poet Umberto Saba in 'Neve' ('Snow'). My poem begins with a loose translation of this line ('Snow that covers us from above, / Cover us more deeply'), allowing its imperative to structure the utterance that follows, as if the repetitive syntax were itself the fulfillment of the wish for more."

BRIDGET LOWE was born in Kansas City, Missouri, in 1981, and currently lives in St. Louis, where she is a lecturer and visiting writer at Washington University. She won the "Discovery" / *Boston Review* prize in 2009 and spent the spring of 2011 as a Fellow at the MacDowell Colony. She graduated from Beloit College and received an MFA in creative writing from Syracuse University in 2009.

Lowe writes: " 'The Pilgrim Is Bridled and Bespectacled' is a love poem from the speaker to the world, two who love each other very much in spite of their differences. The spectacles are significant to me because I have very poor vision and went a long time unable to see properly. When I first put on glasses at fourteen, I felt both enthralled and devastated—the world was so much more (more beautiful, more disappointing) than what I had imagined it to be. This is a poem lamenting

the ocular clarity that the world presents to the bespectacled speaker, and from which the speaker wishes to turn away—but doesn't."

MAURICE MANNING was born in 1966 in Kentucky, where he still lives. He has published four books of poetry: *Lawrence Booth's Book of Visions* (Yale University Press, 2001), *A Companion for Owls* (Houghton Mifflin Harcourt, 2004), *Bucolics* (Houghton Mifflin Harcourt, 2007), and *The Common Man* (Houghton Mifflin Harcourt, 2010). Manning is an associate professor at Indiana University and teaches in the program for writers at Warren Wilson College.

Of "The Complaint against Roney Laswell's Rooster," Manning writes: "A couple of years ago I realized I could not write a lyric poem. Lyricism certainly interested me, but I found I was too tied to a narrative context to feel the real freedom of the lyric. So I devised a short stanza—thirty words long. I gave myself a few other parameters as well: the stanza has six lines and each line has five words; odd-numbered lines are mostly iambic and even-numbered lines are mostly trochaic. This stanza form simply gave me a small space, but happily I've found a lot of wiggle room within it. Brooks Haxton has described this poem and others like it as a 'honky tanka,' which seems about right."

MORTON MARCUS (1936–2009) was a poet, author, editor, teacher, film critic, and activist for the arts. Born in New York City, Mort spent most of his professional life in Santa Cruz, California, and he is strongly associated with its poetry and art community. He published eleven volumes of poetry, a book of translations, a novel, and a memoir. Mort hosted KUSP's *Poetry Show,* hosted film discussion groups at the Nickelodeon Theater, and was the cohost of a television show about film called *Cinema Scene.* More than five hundred of his poems have appeared in literary magazines and anthologies.

JILL MCDONOUGH was born in Hartford, Connecticut, in 1972. Her first book of poems, *Habeas Corpus,* was published by Salt in 2008. The recipient of fellowships from the National Endowment for the Arts, the Fine Arts Work Center, the New York Public Library, and Stanford's Stegner program, she won a Pushcart Prize and a Witter Bynner Fellowship in 2010. She has taught incarcerated college students through Boston University's prison education program since 1999.

McDonough writes: " 'Dear Gaybashers' is about a real-life anonymous sausage-assault, and about one of friendship's best perks. Some

asshole hit me in the neck with a hot dog; it might have been scary if I'd been alone, or if I didn't have anyone I could tell. Instead it was instantly funny, and as we kept talking about it, its various funninesses kept evolving. In the odd aftermath that must always accompany weiner-violence—who knew?—the bright, welcoming Folsom Gulch Bookstore, 'Committed to Pleasure,' was an oasis the homophobes don't get. They also didn't get to go to Annie's Social Club with Rusty and Josey and Bob to drink beer and make dildo, hot dog, and douche-bag jokes all night. Probably they just kept driving around smelling like raw hot dog. We win."

ERIKA MEITNER was born in Queens, New York, in 1975. She is the author of *Inventory at the All-night Drugstore* (2003) and *Makeshift Instructions for Vigilant Girls* (2011), both published by Anhinga Press. Her collection *Ideal Cities* was a 2009 National Poetry Series winner, and was published in 2010 by HarperCollins. She is currently an assistant professor of English at Virginia Tech, where she teaches in the MFA program, and is completing her doctorate in religious studies at the University of Virginia.

Of "Elegy with Construction Sounds, Water, Fish," Meitner writes: "My beloved grandmother, who survived Auschwitz and a late-life leg amputation, and managed to outlive all of her younger sisters, died on Mother's Day in 2008 at the age of ninety-three. With her went Yiddish—her first language, and the language she still used often when she spoke with my mother and aunt. I had just moved, the year before her death, to a tract house development-in-progress in a fairly rural area of southwest Virginia, and everything about the landscape here seemed foreign to me, down to the cracking red clay soil in the yard.

"All summer, I kept thinking of a quote I had stumbled across in 2006, when my grandmother's health first started to decline, in Leon Wieseltier's book *Kaddish.* He was talking about the Galicianer accents the men of his father's generation had: 'These accents are a shorthand for displacement and destruction, for resilience and a multiplicity of resources, for the span of the Jewish journey. I cannot imagine Jewish life without the music of these accents. But soon they will be gone.'

"Some of the lines about Yiddish in the poem come from an analysis written by Maurice Samuel in 1943, as cited by Jonathan Z. Smith in his book *Map Is Not Territory,* which is a book of academic essays on sacred space and time that I was required to read that summer for a comprehensive exam in religious methodology. The point Samuel was making was

that in comparison with other folk languages, Yiddish 'is poor, almost bankrupt . . . in the vocabulary of field and forest and stream.' This elegy was my struggle to find a language for the sounds of grief, which seems as mysterious to me, still, as the flora and fauna of Appalachia."

PAUL MULDOON was born in County Armagh, Northern Ireland, in 1951 and was educated in Armagh and at the Queen's University of Belfast. He is Howard G. B. Clark '21 Professor at Princeton University and chair of the Peter B. Lewis Center for the Arts. His main collections of poetry are *New Weather* (1973), *Mules* (1977), *Why Brownlee Left* (1980), *Quoof* (1983), *Meeting the British* (1987), *Madoc: A Mystery* (1990), *The Annals of Chile* (1994), *Hay* (1998), *Poems 1968–1998* (2001), *Moy Sand and Gravel* (2002), *Horse Latitudes* (2006), and *Maggot* (2010). He was the guest editor of *The Best American Poetry 2005*. He is the poetry editor of *The New Yorker*.

Of "The Side Project," Muldoon writes: "I was thrilled by the prospect of running away and joining a circus for the time it took to write this odd little poem. One of the images that got me going was the idea of waking up 'in a four-poster elephant herd,' while the yoking of that nightmarish idea to the shifting connections between members of the circus who play different roles, including the roles of the speaker of the poem and his bedmate, seemed a fruitful one. The strained relations between the great nineteenth-century ringmasters, Barnum and Forepaugh, carry over into a modern arena. Meanwhile, 'the end of an era' mentioned at the close of the poem refers partly to the fact that 'The Side Project' is the last of a series of longer poems written over the past fifteen years in which, like the members of the circus taking on different roles, the same ninety end-words have rung the changes on a range of emotionally charged themes. It's now time for another tack and tactic."

JUDE NUTTER was born in 1960 in North Yorkshire, England, and grew up near Hannover, in northern Germany. Her first book-length collection, *Pictures of the Afterlife* (Salmon Poetry, Ireland), was published in 2002. *The Curator of Silence* (University of Notre Dame Press), her second collection, won the Ernest Sandeen Prize from the University of Notre Dame and was awarded the 2007 Minnesota Book Award in poetry. A third collection, *I Wish I Had a Heart Like Yours, Walt Whitman* (University of Notre Dame Press), was awarded the 2010 Minnesota Book Award in poetry and voted Poetry Book of the Year by *ForeWord*

Review. She is self-employed and has been teaching in Minneapolis–St. Paul since 1998. In 2004–2005 she spent two months in Antarctica as a participant in the National Science Foundation's Writers and Artists Program.

Born in Houston, Texas, in 1974, JENI OLIN writes: "I am a local & global human rights defender and equality activist. I spend my days making devotional art, writing poetry, and transcribing my pastor's reflections. I spend my evenings doing social justice research and volunteering at an emergency LGBTQI homeless youth shelter in Hell's Kitchen, NYC. I studied at Oxford, Cambridge, and Appalachian State before receiving my BA and MFA degrees in writing and poetics from Naropa University in 1999.

"On a personal note, I am beloved and live in Times Square.

"All my past work is under the name Jeni Olin. My first publication was an Erudite Fangs/Smokeproof Press collaboration called *A Valentine to Frank O'Hara* in March of 1999. My books *Blue Collar Holiday* and *Hold Tight: The Truck Darling Poems* were published by Hanging Loose Press in April 2005 and 2010, respectively. The German press luxbooks published a bilingual edition of my poems in a book titled *Ich habe Angst um meinen Hedgefonds* in March 2008, and Faux Press (Cambridge, MA) published my chapbook *The Pill Book* in April 2008. My poems have recently appeared in *The Portable Boog Reader, The Hat, LIT,* and *Hanging Loose* magazines."

Of "Pillow Talk," Jeni Olin (also known as Truck Darling) writes: "What does one write in a statement about a poem mourning the loss of a companion one later discovered they did not know on some seminal levels and a self-bio of who the author is when one has been asleep for many decades and it is the middle of the night and one is five hours and nine years too late? When I wrote this poem, I had not slept in years??? No, rather: I vehemently believe the human witness holds divine potential.

"I nursed the artist this poem is about, Larry 'Champ' Rivers, as he lived and as he died, and I believe, in all honesty, he taught me how to care for and love. What can I say—growing up publicly can be embarrassing. I made a lot of mistakes, but I do not believe one should ever apologize for love. Also I'm finished with dying. I know my true name and allegiances and past lives, but have no idea what pronouns to use. I only know who holds tomorrow. I'm sort of waking up and getting back to work now. My Christian name is Truck Darling."

ERIC PANKEY was born in Kansas City, Missouri, in 1959. He is a professor of English and the Heritage Chair in Writing at George Mason University. His previous books are *For the New Year* (Atheneum, 1984), *Heartwood* (Atheneum, 1988), *Apocrypha* (Knopf, 1991), *The Late Romances* (Knopf, 1996), *Cenotaph* (Knopf, 2000), *Oracle Figures* (Ausable Press, 2003), *Reliquaries* (Ausable Press, 2005), and *The Pear as One Example: New and Selected Poems 1984–2008* (Ausable Press, 2008). *Dissolve* is forthcoming from Milkweed Editions in 2013.

ALAN MICHAEL PARKER was born in New York in 1961. He is the author of seven collections of poetry, including the forthcoming *Holier than This* (Tupelo Press, 2012), and two novels, including *Whale Man* (WordFarm, 2011). He is also editor of *The Imaginary Poets* (Tupelo Press, 2006), and coeditor of two other volumes of scholarship. He has received the Fineline Prize from the *Mid-American Review* and the Lucille Medwick Memorial Award from the Poetry Society of America. He teaches at Davidson College, where he is professor of English and director of creative writing; he is also a core faculty member in the Queens University low-residency MFA program.

Of "Family Math," Parker writes: "Prior to my son's birth, a friend advised me to pay attention to the smell in the birthing room, if I could remember to do so. He was right. Trying to write about that smell, and thinking about the attempt to characterize different types of experiences, led to the writing of this poem, and to the tallying that inspired the poem's design."

CATHERINE PIERCE was born in Wilmington, Delaware, in 1978. She is the author of *Famous Last Words* (2008), winner of the Saturnalia Books Poetry Prize, and *The Girls of Peculiar,* forthcoming from Saturnalia Books in 2012. She lives in Starkville, Mississippi, where she is codirector of the creative writing program at Mississippi State University.

Of "Postcards from Her Alternate Lives," Pierce writes: "I frequently have this daydream in which I go back to my younger self and say something like, Hey, believe it or not, in fifteen years you'll be [fill in the blank with something inconceivable to the earlier me: a college professor; living in Mississippi; married and a mother; someone who eats avocados and catfish; etc.]. That recurrent daydream prompted me to begin work on a short series of postcard-poems addressed to a self from some other version of that self. For this one, I was thinking about all of the paths I was certain, at one time or another, my life would

take, and how it ended up going somewhere else altogether. Here I let myself imagine, briefly, what those other lives might have been like. By ending on the most disheartening of the scenarios, I intended to make the poem ultimately a happy one—these alternate lives aren't nearly as satisfying or surprising as the one that ended up actually happening."

ROBERT PINSKY was born in Long Branch, New Jersey, in 1940. His *Selected Poems* was published in 2011 by Farrar, Straus and Giroux. His recent anthology, with accompanying audio CD, is *Essential Pleasures*. He has won the Italian Premio Capri, the Harold Washington Award from the city of Chicago, and the *Los Angeles Times* Book Prize for his translation of *The Inferno of Dante*. The videos from his Favorite Poem Project can be viewed at www.favoritepoemproject.org.

Of "Horn," Pinsky writes: "Among the many objects lost by anyone in the course of a life, for me the one most grieved for is a Buescher 'Aristocrat' tenor saxophone: a noble instrument I bought from a soldier-musician stationed at Fort Monmouth, when I was fourteen. I paid for that horn with money (a few hundred dollars that would be thousands today) that I had earned performing, using a lesser instrument, at high school dances, bars, beach clubs, weddings and bar mitzvahs, etc. My Buescher was stolen when I was in college. I still miss it.

"That's a kind of vague background for 'Horn.' More immediately, at the center of the poem is a story I have heard or read somewhere about Charlie Parker. His ear and mind gave him the power to find something worth appreciating in the music played even by a barely competent player: something unique. In the story as I remember it, Parker and his friend walk by the doorway of a New York bar where a journeyman tenor player can be heard playing inside, the anonymous horn man wailing away accompanied by a Hammond organ. (For years, a common blend of instruments.) Parker, instructively, stops on the sidewalk to appreciate something distinctive the hornplayer is doing. He pauses to listen and explain what he hears to his friend.

" 'Horn' gestures toward the idea that work in an art, if it's genuine, will be in some minimal way unique—and yet, in some other way, always a collaboration: a collaboration not only with all the music you have ever heard, and with the centuries of inventors and tinkers who developed the instrument itself, but with all the people who have touched your life, for good or ill. With all of music, great or not so great, or with all of poetry, or at some remove even with all of life: your teacher, your doctor, your optician, and more—in some sense,

everyone is part of what you do in art. Even the son of a bitch bastard who stole my horn in some sense collaborates with me—I hope posthumously, after an embarrassing illness—as I strive to make a poem."

KATHA POLLITT was raised in Brooklyn and has lived most of her life in New York City. She is the author of four books of essays, most recently *Virginity or Death!* (Random House, 2006) and *Learning to Drive and Other Life Stories* (Random House, 2007), and two collections of poetry, *Antarctic Traveller* (Knopf, 1982) and *The Mind-Body Problem* (Random House, 2009). She has won a National Book Critics Circle Award for poetry, two National Magazine Awards for essays and criticism, a National Endowment for the Arts grant, a Guggenheim Fellowship, a Whiting Writers' Award, and in 2010 the American Book Award for Lifetime Achievement. She writes a column on politics and culture for *The Nation* and reviews books for *Slate* and other magazines. She lives in Manhattan with her husband, Steven Lukes.

Pollitt writes: " 'Angels' is a semi-humorous treatment of that perennial theme, the bad fit between reality and possibility. The germ of the idea came from a long-ago visit to the University of the South, where a student told me tradition held that to keep you safe an angel got into your car when you left campus, and stayed there till you returned. You made a certain tapping gesture to summon the angel and to let it go. Sweet for the student, but what about the angel? Was it expected to hang about waiting while you stopped to get a burger? I was struck by the disparity between these magnificent heavenly creatures and the mundane things people ask them to do: give answers on a test, or find lost objects. It must be very disappointing for angels to be asked to use their powers in such trivial ways.

"In my poem, the angels, fed up with doing chores for human beings, hide out in obscurity. They've reached the point where they just want to be left alone, but maybe they have a lot of secret fun, too. They remind me in a way of certain older gay men I knew long ago, rather buttoned-down and formal characters, who had boring day jobs way beneath their abilities, and intense outside passions—jazz, books, theater, romance."

D. A. POWELL was born in Albany, Georgia, in 1963. His books include *Cocktails* (Graywolf, 2004) and *Chronic* (Graywolf, 2009), both finalists for the National Book Critics Circle Award. He is the recipient of the California Book Award, the Lyric Poetry Prize from the Poetry Society

of America, and the Kingsley Tufts Poetry Prize. Powell has taught at Columbia University, Harvard, and the University of Iowa. He is currently the McGee Visiting Writer at Davidson College in North Carolina.

Of "Bugcatching at Twilight," Powell writes: "It kind of speaks for itself, really. The poem is about getting picked up by off-duty military personnel in a parking lot near a park. I guess we've all been there before. It's also about nature, especially in the way that a good grope reminds you of spring. And spring reminds you of fall. And fall reminds you of camouflage. And camouflage gets you right back into the bushes."

GRETCHEN STEELE PRATT was born in Meriden, Connecticut, in 1981. She is the author of one book of poems, *One Island* (Anhinga Press, 2011), which won the 2009 Anhinga Prize for Poetry. She attended the College of Charleston and Purdue University, where she earned an MFA. She lives in Charlotte, North Carolina, with her husband and daughter, and teaches as an adjunct instructor at UNC Charlotte and Wingate University.

Of "To my father on the anniversary of his death," Pratt writes: "I have a recurring dream in which my father comes back to life, but with the understanding that he may die again at any moment. I suspect these dreams had something to do with the impulse behind this poem; it was one of those rare, lucky experiences when the poem comes all at once and seems to write itself.

"This poem anticipates a later poem in *One Island* that begins with a question from Neruda's *Book of Questions*: 'And does the father who lives in your dreams die again when you awaken?'"

JAMES RICHARDSON was born in Bradenton, Florida, in 1950 and has for the past thirty years taught poetry at Princeton University. His most recent books are *By the Numbers: Poems and Aphorisms* (Copper Canyon, 2010), which was a finalist for the National Book Award; *Interglacial: New and Selected Poems and Aphorisms* (Ausable Press, 2004), a finalist for the National Book Critics Circle Award; *Vectors: Aphorisms and Ten-Second Essays* (Ausable Press, 2001); and *How Things Are* (Carnegie Mellon, 2000). His work has appeared in *The Best American Poetry* (2001, 2005, 2009, 2010).

Of "Even More Aphorisms and Ten-Second Essays from Vectors 3.0," Richardson writes: "My favorite dictionary says aphorisms are 'tersely phrased statements of truths or opinions.' Mine seem to me, a

little less solemnly, part proverb, part joke: their apparent confidence is play or speculation, their method second-guessing and self-editing. I think of them as Literary Doritos, since they're so hard to stop writing. With eight hundred or so in print, I have a minor fantasy of assembling enough for a collection called *Kilobyte: 1024 Aphorisms and Ten-Second Essays.*"

ANNE MARIE ROONEY was born in New York City in 1985. She has worked as an artist's model, an ESL teacher, and an indexer, and was most recently a lecturer at Cornell University, where she earned her MFA in poetry. She is the recipient of the *Iowa Review* Award, the *Gulf Coast* Poetry Prize, and the Amy Award, given by *Poets & Writers* to young female poets living and working in New York. Her debut collection is *Spitshine* (Carnegie Mellon University Press, 2011).

Of "What my heart is turning," Rooney writes: "I wrote this poem the summer after I graduated from college, a sort of limbo time when I had no idea what I was going to do, much less write. After spending too much time in writing workshops, I'd begun to question—am still questioning, actually—just how much I could get away with in a poem. I want to push up against these limits, to lick their faces, tenderize them, make them scared to walk alone at night. Can I say, 'I love you'? No? Can I talk about my capital-h 'Heart,' unironically, even sweetly? Because I am perpetually in love, head-over-heels-messy, everywhere at once and with too many words to speak it. I want to talk about these feelings honestly, dangerously, without leaning on pretension to mask lazy writing, but without shying away from the obscure or possibly alienating, either. Perhaps this is why I like sonnets so much (though 'What my heart is turning' is not a sonnet): in their old and inevitable reason, they reveal their artifice by almost making love to it. I also love sonnets for a slew of other, as ever, messier reasons—ask me.'"

MARY RUEFLE was born in McKeesport, Pennsylvania, in 1952. Her latest book is *Selected Poems* (Wave Books, 2010). She is also the author of a book of prose, *The Most of It* (Wave Books, 2008), and an artist who erases, treats, and extra-illustrates nineteenth-century books (maryruefle.com). She lives in Vermont.

Of "Provenance," Ruefle writes: "The poem is a straightforward, factual chronicle of events from my childhood; in attempting to write about it, my opening sentence matched, word for word, the first stanza of the poem—I saw that and decided to stop!"

DAVID ST. JOHN was born in Fresno, California, in 1949, and now lives in Venice Beach, California. He teaches at the University of Southern California. He is the author of nine collections of poetry, most recently *The Face: A Novella in Verse* (HarperCollins, 2004), for which he has written the libretto for the opera *The Face,* composed by Donald Crockett. *Study for the World's Body: New & Selected Poems* (HarperCollins, 1994) was nominated for the National Book Award in poetry. His forthcoming collection, *The Auroras,* will appear from HarperCollins in January 2012.

St. John writes: " 'Ghost Aurora' is one section of the twelve-part title poem of *The Auroras* (which comprises the final part of the book). 'Ghost Aurora' is perhaps the explicit section of several that address the ancient legacy of poetic calling, poetic vocation. All of the sections are to some degree speculative, philosophical, and metaphysical in their desires, but I think 'Ghost Aurora' is the most delicate in its foregrounding of the ephemeral nature of the act of writing poems. So I suppose it can also be seen as a kind of *ars poetica.*"

MARY JO SALTER was born in Grand Rapids, Michigan, in 1954. She is Andrew W. Mellon Professor at the Writing Seminars at Johns Hopkins University. Her six volumes of poems include *Henry Purcell in Japan* (1985), *Unfinished Painting* (1989), *Sunday Skaters* (1995), *A Kiss in Space* (1999), *Open Shutters* (2004), and *A Phone Call to the Future: New and Selected Poems* (2008), all published by Knopf. She has also published a children's book, *The Moon Comes Home* (Knopf, 1989), and is a coeditor of the fourth and fifth editions of *The Norton Anthology of Poetry* (W. W. Norton & Co., 1996 and 2005). She edited *The Selected Poems of Amy Clampitt,* published by Knopf in 2010.

Of "The Afterlife," Salter writes: "Miniatures have always obsessed me. Representation—our ambitious attempt at mirroring 'reality'—is inherently fascinating, but most thrilling (at least for me) when the mimetic scale is seriously off. And as for death—who isn't obsessed with that?

"It feels retrospectively inevitable, then, that someday I'd try my hand at writing about *shabti*: the pint-sized servants, made of clay or stone, who labored in the crypts into eternity for dead-and-buried noble Egyptians. Stumbling upon the exceptional collection of Egyptian crypt-dwellers at the Oriental Museum at the University of Chicago, I was enchanted by the homely practicality of their tasks: brewing beer, baking bread. At the same time, the tomb became for me a sort of philo-

sophical hall of mirrors. As I represented in words an artist painting the wall of a crypt with an image of an artist making *shabti*, who in turn represented humans like me, I began to feel dizzy. More grateful, too, for life—for a simple snowfall, for instance. The poem ends with an exit from the museum-tomb and into the blessed daylight. (But why does the snow look like dust?)

"The poem is dedicated to my daughter Hilary Leithauser, who helped me look more closely."

JAMES SCHUYLER (1923–1991) was born in Chicago, Illinois. His books of poems include *Freely Espousing* (1969), *The Crystal Lithium* (1972), *Hymn to Life* (1974), *The Morning of the Poem* (1980), and *A Few Days* (1985). *The Morning of the Poem* received the Pulitzer Prize. Farrar, Straus and Giroux published both his *Collected Poems* and *Selected Poems*. A mainstay of the New York School of poets, Schuyler collaborated with John Ashbery on a novel (*A Nest of Ninnies*) and was coeditor of *Locus Solus* magazine. Like an expert draftsman who with three or four strokes can suggest a human face, Schuyler wrote "skinny poems"—pastoral in setting, exact in description, terse in expression—that can bring a landscape to life. In other poems, such as the title poem of *A Few Days,* Schuyler favored a conversational style and brought a touching intimacy and exuberance to the depiction of the erotic life.

"The Smallest" is from a book of previously uncollected poems, *Other Flowers,* edited by James Meetze and Simon Pettet from folders found in the Mandeville Special Collections Library at the University of California, San Diego. This is Schuyler's fifth appearance in *The Best American Poetry* and the third time a posthumous poem was selected. For the 2001 volume, Robert Hass tapped "Along Overgrown Paths," which the series editor had unearthed in John Ashbery's archive at Harvard's Houghton Library. "Having My Say-So" appeared in the 2010 volume edited by Amy Gerstler.

CHARLES SIMIC is a poet, essayist, and translator. He was born in Yugoslavia in 1938 and immigrated to the United States in 1954. His first poems were published in 1959, when he was twenty-one. In 1961 he was drafted into the U.S. Army, and in 1966 he earned his bachelor's degree from New York University while working at night to cover the cost of tuition. Since 1967, he has published twenty books of his own poetry, seven books of essays, a memoir, and numerous translations of

French, Serbian, Croatian, Macedonian, and Slovenian poetry. He has received many literary awards, including the Pulitzer Prize, the Griffin Prize, the MacArthur Fellowship, and the Wallace Stevens Award. His recent collections of poems are *The Voice at 3:00 A.M.* (Harcourt, 2003), *That Little Something* (Harcourt, 2009), and *Master of Disguises* (Harcourt, 2010). Simic is an emeritus professor at the University of New Hampshire, where he has taught since 1973. He was the poet laureate of the United States in 2007–2008. He had two other new books in 2009, *Renegade* (George Braziller, Inc.) and *The Monster Loves His Labyrinth* (Copper Canyon Press), selections from notebooks. He was the guest editor of *The Best American Poetry 1992.*

Of "Nineteen Thirty-Eight," Simic writes: "This poem of mine I ought to have dedicated to Google. I was thinking one day about the year of my birth and all the things that were going on in the world while I was in my crib, so, I thought, let's see if I can write a poem about that. Of course, I needed the list of things that happened that year and with the help of the Internet provided myself in short order with more information than I could ever use. It took me over a year to get it in this shape, because I kept changing my mind what to put in and what to leave out."

MATTHEW BUCKLEY SMITH was born in Atlanta, Georgia, in 1982. He studied drama at the University of Georgia and poetry at the Johns Hopkins University. He is currently studying playwriting at the Catholic University of America. He teaches high school literature and undergraduate creative writing. He lives in Baltimore with his wife, Joanna Pearson.

Of "Nowhere," Smith writes: "Steve Sigur taught math at the Paideia School in Atlanta, where I attended high school. He stood about six foot six, wore a belly-length beard, and dressed most days in a misbuttoned oxford cloth shirt and swimming trunks. Steve played over a dozen musical instruments and had memorized hundreds of lines of Yeats's poetry. He was working with a professor at Princeton on a book about triangles when he died. For years after I graduated, Steve and I would meet for lunch and conversation, sometimes at the traditional lunchtime, sometimes at three in the morning. He believed in living without ulterior motives and seemed generally to have put this belief into practice. Shortly before I wrote 'Nowhere,' I joined scores of Steve's former students in writing him a final letter. He had taught my brother in the spring semester and believed that he would be returning

in the fall. I wrote the poem that summer because I could think of no consolation for his death. I still can't."

PATRICIA SMITH was born in Chicago, Illinois, in 1955. She is the author of five books of poetry, including *Blood Dazzler,* a 2008 National Book Award finalist chronicling the emotional, physical, and psychological toll exacted by Hurricane Katrina; and *Teahouse of the Almighty,* a National Poetry Series selection and winner of the first-ever Hurston/ Wright Legacy Award in Poetry. She also wrote the history *Africans in America* (the companion book to the PBS series) and the children's book *Janna and the Kings,* which won Lee & Low Books' New Voices Award. A choreoplay based on *Blood Dazzler,* cocreated by former Urban Bush Women choreographer Paloma McGregor, recently debuted off-Broadway in NYC. In addition, Smith has written and starred in three one-woman shows, including one directed by Derek Walcott. She has been awarded a Lannan Foundation residency, a New York Foundation for the Arts fellowship, and a Pushcart Prize. She is a Cave Canem faculty member and a four-time individual champion of the National Poetry Slam, the most successful poet in the competition's history. A graduate of the Stonecoast MFA program, Smith is currently a professor of English and creative writing at the City University of New York/ College of Staten Island.

Smith writes: "I write in a fever, usually after wasting an inordinate amount of time being romanced by all the reasons I CAN'T do something—be it harness a huge emotion or work in a particular metrical form. In the case of 'Motown Crown,' both these issues were on the table. Motown music was an insanely powerful influence during my formative years—in fact, all of my ideas about life, loss, and romance were pretty much defined by whatever Motown song was out at the time. (I'm sure it was my youthful imagination, but when I was about ten or eleven, there seemed to be a song hitting the charts every twenty minutes or so. So to say I was on constant emotional overdose is putting it mildly.) I wanted to pay tribute to the music, especially from my perspective as a wizened adult, but getting my head around the topic proved difficult.

"I fell in love with the possibilities of prosody and meter while pursuing an MFA. During one semester after I had joined the faculty, the visiting poet-in-residence was Marilyn Nelson, reigning diva of the sonnet crown.

"I love the crown. I love its quirky math, its illuminating repetitions,

its insistent song. Dazzled by such talent in such close vicinity, I was an awed babbler: *I wanna write a crown like you, Marilyn I wanna write a crown like you, Marilyn I wanna write a crown like you Marilyn,* until her sigh and arched brow sent me scuttering elsewhere. I'm convinced that merely sharing air with her finally pushed me toward the writing.

"Once I decided that *it was time,* I wrote the crown in a relentlessly driven stupor in about three and a half hours. I had a reading that evening and had made a rash but unflinching promise to myself that the crown would be ready in time. It was decidedly less lyrical than it appears here. In the months after its creation, I visited the crown often. Revision was like walking into the house of an old friend, each time rearranging the furniture a little.

"Now it looks like we're both ready to receive company."

GERALD STERN was born in Pittsburgh, Pennsylvania, in 1925, and was educated at the University of Pittsburgh and Columbia University. He is the author of fifteen books of poetry, including, most recently, *Save the Last Dance* (W. W. Norton & Co., 2008) and *Everything Is Burning* (W. W. Norton & Co., 2005), as well as *This Time: New and Selected Poems,* which won the 1998 National Book Award. The paperback of his personal essays, *What I Can't Bear Losing,* was published in the fall of 2009 by Trinity University Press. He was awarded the 2005 Wallace Stevens Award by the Academy of American Poets and is currently a chancellor of the Academy of American Poets. He is retired from the University of Iowa Writers' Workshop. *Early Collected: Poems from 1965–1992* was published by W. W. Norton in spring 2010.

Stern writes: "Essentially, 'Dream IV' is an antiwar poem, but it takes into account the Jewish vision of and participation in war, especially in the light of the prophets, even if they're not, as such, mentioned. I think I rather 'lumbered in' to the poem, starting with just a feeling, probably of anxiety, and moved ahead with more clarity and purpose after line seven and the mention of 'Jubus.' Why I was, in line four, choosing a Nobel laureate, and for what purpose, I have no idea, nor did I know I was choosing among Israelis, nor did I know if I was choosing *among* already crowned laureates or if I (of all people) was actually choosing, *crowning,* a new one. Their phone call is scary and insidious, but I respond in anger (and humor). In my first version I said 'Jew-Bu' but didn't like the specificity, although I am talking about Jewish Buddhists, common as we know, or not uncommon. The rest of the poem is a commentary of sorts on the book of Numbers (my version) and

a reference to German Jews and their participation (in war), including Einstein and Kissinger, the atom bomb and 'fusion,' and the ugly and stupid role of Kissinger, certainly a German Jew. It ends with the hopeful (hilarious) notion of 'fighting with air.' I am not condemning Germans, German Jews, or Israelis. Heschel was a German Jew as was Oppenheimer. So was Buber, who ended up in Jerusalem. I am just letting the ax fall where it may. What *I* like most about the poem is its simultaneous 'avoidance' and 'clarity'; its secrecy; its odd humor; its clear-cut ending. I like going back to air; if not that, then at least paper."

BIANCA STONE was born in Burlington, Vermont, in 1983. She is the daughter of the novelist Abigail Stone and granddaughter of the poet Ruth Stone. She completed her MFA at New York University's creative writing program in 2009 and is the author of the chapbook *Someone Else's Wedding Vows* from Argos Books (2010). She works as a literary assistant at New York University and is coeditor of the independent press Monk Books. Besides writing poetry, she is also a visual artist and freelance illustrator and is currently working on a collaborative book with Anne Carson, illustrating Carson's translation of *Antigone* (New Directions, 2012). Her blog is called *Poetry Comics:* http://whoisthatsupposedtobe .blogspot.com/. She lives in Brooklyn.

Stone writes: "I wrote 'Pantoum for the Imperceptible' as a part of a series called 'Parable Poems,' which were not actually allegorical or moralistic. Instead, I wanted to explore the idea of parable as something we create in our everyday interactions with what's around us and our relationships. The speaker, in her obsession with the landscape and absent lover, moves to create a parable in order to distance herself emotionally. I remember when I was writing this pantoum, I was thinking a lot about bacteria and prokaryote microorganisms and how human flora performs tasks for the body. I was fascinated with these truly ancient beings, imagining that they might have some alien sway in human decision making. My limited knowledge of science allowed me to have fun with the concept.

"This poem began when I spent some time alone in my grandmother's house in Goshen, Vermont, after graduating college, in hopes of staving off the property's deterioration. Moving to New York City shortly after my defeat, I wrote the parable poems, consumed with my experience. In this series of poems (and in many of my poems), I feel a strong connection to certain landscapes: the literal landscape and the body's landscape have an overwhelming presence in this pantoum. The

longing and frustration in the speaker is translated through her interactions with the elements that surround her. In the frustration of failure, I wanted the speaker to blame the *imperceptible* for everything. At the end of the poem the speaker realizes that even if she has been abandoned by a lover, she is never able to escape her own living body, comprised of seemingly intelligent and cunning microorganisms. What is living within her and around her confirms that she is never actually *alone*. In a sense, I was toying with the idea of religion. Instead of God always being present, it is science that proves you are never alone."

MARK STRAND was born in Summerside, Prince Edward Island, Canada, in 1934. He lives in New York City and teaches at Columbia University. He won the 1999 Pulitzer Prize for *Blizzard of One*. He is the author of a book of stories, *Mr. and Mrs. Baby,* and two monographs on painters (William Bailey and Edward Hopper). He was chosen as poet laureate of the United States in 1990 and was guest editor of *The Best American Poetry 1991.*

Strand writes: "The Poem of the Spanish Poet" began as an attempt to write a song in the manner of some of Lorca's songs. But since I was writing only short prose pieces and wanted only prose pieces in my next book, I concocted a prose surround for it. It's as simple as that."

MARY JO THOMPSON was born in Minneapolis, Minnesota, in 1949. She was educated at the University of Minnesota and at Antioch University New England before beginning her career as a public school teacher on an island off the coast of Maine. She is the lead author of a handbook on integrating the arts in education, *Artful Teaching and Learning,* published in 2005 by the Perpich Center for Arts Education, a Minnesota agency. She works as an arts integration specialist with the Minneapolis Public Schools. In 2009, on her sixtieth birthday, she received an MFA from Warren Wilson College. Her manuscript of poems is titled *Stunt Heart.*

Of "Thirteen Months," Thompson writes: "When I began at Warren Wilson, my advisor, Rick Barot, took a close look at the work I'd submitted with my application and duly noted that I was struggling to deal with difficult personal material. In fact, while trying to avoid falling into the trap of overdetermining the poems, I'd overcompensated. Barot reminded me that Emily Dickinson may have written 'Tell the Truth, but tell it Slant,' but she hadn't said, 'Be Oblique.' He taught me that messy material begged a countervailing form, some kind of container. I read and wrote nothing but sonnets that whole semester. Sure enough,

by counting lines and syllables—while also aiming to make an argument that turned somewhere near the poem's end—I found the detachment I needed. It was only as I reluctantly came to the sonnet that I saw how rules can liberate, and 'Thirteen Months' began to take shape.

"I dedicate the poem, with love, to all of my teachers, and to the members of my brilliant writing group who have seen me through not only thirteen months, but sixteen years."

NATASHA TRETHEWEY is the author of *Beyond Katrina: A Meditation on the Mississippi Gulf Coast* (University of Georgia Press, 2010), and three collections of poetry, *Domestic Work* (Graywolf, 2000), *Bellocq's Ophelia* (Graywolf, 2002), and *Native Guard* (Houghton Mifflin, 2006), for which she was awarded the Pulitzer Prize. A new collection of poems, *Thrall*, is forthcoming from Houghton Mifflin Harcourt in 2012. She is the recipient of NEA, Guggenheim, Bunting, and Rockefeller Fellowships. At Emory University she is professor of English and holds the Phillis Wheatley Distinguished Chair in Poetry.

Of "Elegy," Trethewey writes: "A few years ago my father and I took a trip to his native Canada to go salmon fishing in New Brunswick on the Miramichi River. He is also a poet, and among the poems he has written about me is one that includes another river we visited when I was a small child in Mississippi."

LEE UPTON was born in St. Johns, Michigan, in 1953. Her twelfth book is a prose meditation, *Swallowing the Sea: On Writing and Ambition, Boredom, Purity, & Secrecy,* and is forthcoming in 2012 from Tupelo Press. She has written a novella, *The Guide to the Flying Island* (Miami University Press, 2009); five books of poetry, including *Undid in the Land of Undone* (New Issues, 2007); and four books of literary criticism. She is a professor of English and writer-in-residence at Lafayette College.

Of "Drunk at a Party," Upton writes: "Poetry has disordered my mind—or reoriented my mind—since I was a child. Isn't poetry about alcohol an intoxicant that wants to reflect on other intoxicants? I lead such a quiet life that I can't remember the last time I was drunk. I hardly remember the last time I was at a party. Maybe that party doesn't even qualify as a party, given that it was a reception."

DAVID WAGONER was born in Massillon, Ohio, in 1926. He grew up in Whiting, Indiana, and has lived in or near Seattle since 1954. He has published eighteen books of poems, most recently *A Map of the Night*

(University of Illinois Press, 2008). Copper Canyon Press will publish *After the Point of No Return* in 2012. He has also published ten novels, one of which, *The Escape Artist,* was made into a movie by Francis Ford Coppola. He won the Lilly Prize in 1991 and has won six yearly prizes from *Poetry* (Chicago). He was a chancellor of the Academy of American Poets for twenty-three years. He edited *Poetry Northwest* from 1966 to its end in 2002. He is professor emeritus of English at the University of Washington and teaches in the low-residency MFA program of the Whidbey Island Writers Workshop. He was the guest editor of *The Best American Poetry 2009.*

Of "Thoreau and the Lightning," Wagoner writes: "Henry David Thoreau wrote about many encounters with plants, birds, animals, men, and phenomena in the natural world in his *Journal,* and only a small percentage of them appeared in his published books and essays. His poetry seldom dealt with such specific material. It was rigidly formal and non-colloquial and traditional and metrically 'correct.' Again and again in his *Journal* I've found what seem to me very like the kinds of notes I make for many of my own poems, so a number of times I've tried to finish what I feel Thoreau left undone. 'Thoreau and the Lightning' is one of those efforts."

ROSANNA WARREN was born in Fairfield, Connecticut, in 1953. She received a BA in painting and comparative literature from Yale University, and an MA in creative writing from the Johns Hopkins University. Her recent books include *Ghost in a Red Hat* (poems, 2011), *Fables of the Self: Studies in Lyric Poetry* (2008), and *Departure* (poems, 2003), all from W. W. Norton & Co. With Stephen Scully she published a verse translation of the Euripides play *Suppliant Women* (Oxford University Press, 1995).

Of "The Latch," Warren writes: "I try to keep in mind Ezra Pound's dictum, 'The natural object is always the adequate symbol.' In this poem, the natural object is the broken door lock, and I hoped that by contemplating it steadily I could imply a larger human story. Larger, in the sense of being human, not mechanical, and also expanding back in time (eighty-three years) to suggest the long chain of events in which individual lives and sorrows take their place and meanings. It also matters that the poem is a single sentence, whose unwinding mimics the patient work of the helpful neighbor, the work of the poet composing, and the sense of story itself as a process."

RACHEL WETZSTEON was born in New York City in 1967. She earned a bachelor's degree from Yale, a master's from Johns Hopkins, and a PhD from Columbia. She taught at the Unterberg Poetry Center of the 92nd Street Y and at William Paterson University and served as poetry editor of *The New Republic*. Her books of poetry are *The Other Stars* (Penguin, 1994), *Home and Away* (Penguin, 1998), *Sakura Park* (Persea, 2006), and *Silver Roses* (Persea, 2011). She also wrote a critical study entitled *Influential Ghosts: A Study of Auden's Sources* (Routledge, 2007). Wetzsteon died in New York City in 2009.

RICHARD WILBUR was born in New York City in 1921. His father was a portrait painter, and his mother came from a long line of journalists. A graduate of Amherst College (class of '42), he saw action in World War II with the 36th Infantry Division, and returned to become a professor of English, teaching at Harvard, Wellesley, Wesleyan, Smith, and Amherst. With his wife of sixty-four years, he had four children and three grandchildren. Beginning in 1947, he published many books of poems, translations, essays, and show lyrics, of which the most recent are *Collected Poems 1943–2004* (Harcourt, 2004), *Anterooms* (Harcourt, 2010), and three translations from Corneille—*The Theatre of Illusion* (2007), *Le Cid* (2009), and *The Liar* (2009).

Of "Ecclesiastes II:I," Wilbur writes: "A correspondent delighted me by saying that this is not only a poem but a *midrash*. The poem uses the haiku as a stanza, rhyming the first and third lines. It is a form that offers both fluency and emphasis."

C. K. WILLIAMS was born in Newark, New Jersey, in 1936. His most recent books are *Collected Poems*, published in 2006 by Farrar, Straus and Giroux; *Wait* (2010), also published by Farrar, Straus and Giroux; and a prose study of Walt Whitman, *On Whitman*, published by Princeton University Press in 2010. He has also recently published two children's books, *How the Nobble Was Finally Found*, and *A Not Scary Story About Big Scary Things*, both brought out by Houghton Mifflin Harcourt. He won the Pulitzer Prize in 2000 for *Repair*. He teaches at Princeton University.

Of "A Hundred Bones," Williams writes: "I've become fascinated by how many moments of time are in us at once: our own experience, present and past, our imaginings, our reading, our history, our long-gone emotions and thoughts. When I thought that I'd lived through

World War II, even though I was very young, I decided to try to account for how much of that period was still within me, and how it had resonated through the rest of my personal and creative life.

"I'd also long loved Bashō's statement about poetry, which is worth quoting in its entirety. Noboyuki Yuasa's translation appears in *The Essential Haiku: Versions of Bashō, Buson, and Issa,* edited by Robert Hass.

In this mortal frame of mine, which is made of a hundred bones and nine orifices, there is something, and this something can be called, for lack of a better name, a windswept spirit, for it is much like thin drapery that is torn and swept away by the slightest stirring of the wind. This something in me took to writing poetry years ago, merely to amuse itself at first, but finally making it its lifelong business. It must be admitted, however, that there were times when it sank into such dejection that it was almost ready to drop its pursuit, or again times when it was so puffed up with pride that it exulted in vain victories over others. Indeed, ever since it began to write poetry, it has never found peace with itself, always wavering between doubts of one kind or another. At one time it wanted to gain security by entering the service of a court, at another it wished to measure the depth of its ignorance by trying to be a scholar, but it was prevented from either by its unquenchable love of poetry. The fact is, it knows no other art than the art of writing poetry, and therefore it hangs on to it more or less blindly.

"'A Hundred Bones' grew from all this."

DAVID WOJAHN was born in St. Paul, Minnesota, in 1953. His eighth collection of poetry, *World Tree,* was published by the University of Pittsburgh Press earlier this year. He has received fellowships from the National Endowment for the Arts and the Guggenheim Foundation. His previous collection of poetry, *Interrogation Palace: Selected Poems 1982–2004,* was published by the University of Pittsburgh Press in 2006 and won the Folger Shakespeare Library's O. B. Hardison Award. He teaches at Virginia Commonwealth University and in the MFA in Writing Program of Vermont College.

Wojahn writes: " 'Mix Tape' mainly involves some bittersweet memories—a common subject for poetry. The poem also recalls the 1980s, a low dishonest decade, and references music and other elements

of pop culture from the time. Ronald Reagan makes a brief appearance, a president who in my memory was a very pernicious and polarizing figure. And, since the poem is about memory, it also seems to be about dead formats—in this case cassette tapes and Walkmen. As a boomer, I sometimes feel that my life is composed in no small measure of dead formats."

CHARLES WRIGHT was born in Pickwick Dam, Tennessee, in 1935. He lives in Charlottesville, Virginia, and has recently retired from teaching at the University of Virginia. *Black Zodiac* (Farrar, Straus and Giroux, 1997) won the Pulitzer Prize. His book *Outtakes* was published in 2010 by Sarabande, and *Bye-and-Bye: Selected Late Poems* was published in 2011 by Farrar, Straus and Giroux. He was guest editor of *The Best American Poetry 2008.*

Wright writes: "About 'Toadstools,' there is very little to say. One morning a couple of years ago, I noticed they had come up overnight. I was in Montana, walking to my writing cabin, Xanadu, and when I got inside and sat down at my desk, the poem just happened, exactly as you see it here, and I typed it up and stuck it in my summer folder. As for toadstools themselves, I have no emotional connection to them whatsoever, but I do keep my distance."

STEPHEN YENSER has published *The Fire in All Things* (LSU Press, 1992), which won the Walt Whitman Award from the Academy of American Poets, and *Blue Guide* (University of Chicago Press, 2006). He has written three critical books, the latest of which is *A Boundless Field: American Poetry at Large,* and he is coeditor of five volumes of James Merrill's work. He is distinguished professor and director of creative writing at UCLA and lives in Los Angeles.

Yenser writes: "As some readers of 'Cycladic Idyll' will soon realize, the friend absent in the poem is James Merrill, who helped me and many others get a foothold in Greek culture. Although on a couple of occasions, he composed footnotes (not endnotes) that he meant to be extensions of their poems, like aerial roots of some fig trees, James felt that the poem should explain as much of itself as it could, and I am inclined to agree."

MAGAZINES WHERE THE POEMS
WERE FIRST PUBLISHED

32 Poems, eds. Deborah Ager and John Poch. PO Box 5824, Hyattsville, MD 20782.

AGNI, poetry ed. Lynne Potts. Boston University, 236 Bay State Road, Boston, MA 02215.

The American Poetry Review, eds. Stephen Berg, David Bonanno, and Elizabeth Scanlon. 1700 Sansom Street, Suite 800, Philadelphia, PA 19103.

The American Scholar, ed. Langdon Hammer. 1606 New Hampshire Avenue NW, Washington, DC 20009.

The Atlantic, poetry ed. David Barber. The Watergate, 600 New Hampshire Avenue NW, Washington, DC 20037.

At Length, poetry ed. Jonathan Farmer. www.atlengthmag.com.

The Believer, poetry ed. Dominic Luxford. 849 Valencia Street, San Francisco, CA 94110.

Beloit Poetry Journal, eds. Lee Sharkey and John Rosenwald. PO Box 151, Farmington, ME 04938.

Black Warrior Review, ed. Jenny Gropp Hess. www.bwr.ua.edu.

Boston Review, poetry eds. Timothy Donnelly and Benjamin Paloff. 35 Medford Street, Suite 302, Somerville, MA 02143.

Boulevard, ed. Richard Burgin. 6614 Clayton Road, PO Box 325, Richmond Heights, MO 63117.

Cave Wall, eds. Rhett Iseman Trull and Jeff Trull. PO Box 29546, Greensboro, NC 27429-9546.

The Cincinnati Review, poetry ed. Don Bogen. PO Box 210069, Cincinnati, OH 45221-0069.

Court Green, eds. Tony Trigilio and David Trinidad. Columbia College Chicago, 600 South Michigan Avenue, Chicago, IL 60605.

Denver Quarterly, ed. Bin Ramke. University of Denver, Department of English, 2000 E. Asbury, Denver, CO 80208.

DMQ Review, ed. Sally Ashton. www.dmqreview.com.

Ecotone, poetry ed. Kyle Simmons. Department of Creative Writing, University of North Carolina, Wilmington, 601 S. College Road, Wilmington, NC 28403-5938.

Green Mountains Review, poetry ed. Elizabeth Powell. 337 College Hill, Johnson, VT 05656.

Gulf Coast, poetry eds. Samuel Amadon, Liz Countryman, and Janine Joseph. Department of English, University of Houston, Houston, TX 77204-3013.

Hanging Loose, ed. Robert Hershon. 231 Wyckoff Street, Brooklyn, NY 11217.

The Iowa Review, poetry ed. Nick Twemlow, associate ed. Emily Liebowitz. 308 EPB, The University of Iowa, Iowa City, IA 52242.

Iron Horse Literary Review, poetry ed. Carrie Jerrell. Texas Tech University, English Department, Mail Stop 43091, Lubbock, TX 79409.

jubilat, eds. Cathy Park Hong and Evie Shockley. Department of English, 452 Bartlett Hall, University of Massachusetts, Amherst, MA 01003-0515.

The Kenyon Review, poetry ed. David Baker. www.kenyonreview.org.

LIT, poetry ed. Ben Mirov. The New School, Writing Program, Room 514, 66 W. 12th Street, New York, NY 10011.

The Literary Review, poetry eds. Renée Ashley and David Daniel. Fairleigh Dickinson University, 285 Madison Avenue, Madison, NJ 07940.

London Review of Books, ed. Mary-Kay Wilmers. 28 Little Russell Street, London WC1A 2HN, UK.

Maggy, eds. Adam Fitzgerald, Alina Gregorian, and Allison Power. www.maggypoetry.com.

McSweeney's, ed. Dave Eggers. www.mcsweeneys.net.

Michigan Quarterly Review, ed. Jonathan Freedman. 0576 Rackham Bldg., 915 E. Washington Street, Ann Arbor, MI 48109-1070.

The Nation, poetry ed. Peter Gizzi. 33 Irving Place, New York, NY 10003.

The New Criterion, poetry ed. David Yezzi. 900 Broadway, Suite 602, New York, NY 10003.

New England Review, poetry ed. C. Dale Young. Middlebury College, Middlebury, VT 05753.

New Ohio Review, ed. Jill Allyn Rosser. English Department, 360 Ellis Hall, Ohio University, Athens, OH 45701.

New South, poetry ed. James Thomas Miller. Campus Box 1894, Georgia State University, MSC 8R0322, Unit 8, Atlanta, GA 30303-3083.

The New Yorker, poetry ed. Paul Muldoon. 4 Times Square, New York, NY 10036.

The New York Quarterly, ed. Raymond Hammond. PO Box 2015, Old Chelsea Station, New York, NY 10113.

The Paris Review, poetry ed. Robyn Creswell. 62 White Street, New York, NY 10013.

Ploughshares, poetry ed. John Skoyles; guest ed. Elizabeth Strout. Emerson College, 120 Boylston Street, Boston, MA 02116-4624.

Poetry, ed. Christian Wiman. 444 N. Michigan Avenue, Suite 1850, Chicago, IL 60611-4034.

Poetry Daily, eds. Rob Anderson, Diane Boller, and Don Selby. www.poems.com.

Post Road, poetry eds. Mark Conway, Anne McCarty, Nicolette Nicola, Jeffrey Shotts, and Lissa Warren. 140 Commonwealth Avenue, Carney Room 334, Chestnut Hill, MA 02467.

Prairie Schooner, ed. Hilda Raz. 201 Andrews Hall, PO Box 880334, Lincoln, NE 68588-0334.

Rattle, ed. Timothy Green, 12411 Ventura Boulevard, Studio City, CA 91604.

River Styx, ed. Richard Newman. 3547 Olive Street, Suite 107, St. Louis, MO 63103.

Salmagundi, eds. Robert Boyers and Peg Boyers. Skidmore College, 815 N. Broadway, Saratoga Springs, NY 12866.

Sentence, ed. Brian Clements. Box 7, Western Connecticut State University, 181 White Street, Danbury, CT 06810.

The Sewanee Review, ed. George Core. University of the South, 735 University Avenue, Sewanee, TN 37383-1000.

Southwest Review, ed. Willard Spiegelman. PO Box 750374, Dallas, TX 75275-0374.

Sycamore Review, poetry eds. Mario Chard and Josh Wild. Purdue University, Department of English, 500 Oval Drive, West Lafayette, IN 47907.

upstreet, poetry ed. Jessica Greenbaum. www.upstreet-mag.org.

The Virginia Quarterly Review, ed. Ted Genoways. www.vqronline.org.

The Yale Review, ed. J. D. McClatchy. Yale University, PO Box 208243, New Haven, CT 06520-8243.

ACKNOWLEDGMENTS

The series editor thanks Mark Bibbins for his invaluable assistance. I am grateful as well to John Ashbery, Patricia Carlin, Laura Cronk, James Cummins, George Green, Stacey Harwood, Robert Hass, Elizabeth Howort, Kathleen Ossip, Stephanie Paterik, Michael Schiavo, Paul Violi, and David Wagoner. Warm thanks go, as always, to Glen Hartley and Lynn Chu of Writers' Representatives, and to Alexis Gargagliano, my editor, as well as David Stanford Burr, Erich Hobbing, Kelsey Smith, and Daniel Cuddy of Scribner.

Grateful acknowledgment is made of the magazines in which these poems first appeared and the magazine editors who selected them. A sincere attempt has been made to locate all copyright holders. Unless otherwise noted, copyright to the poems is held by the individual poets.

Elizabeth Alexander: "Rally" from *Crave Radiance.* © 2010 by Elizabeth Alexander. Reprinted by permission of Graywolf Press. Also appeared in *The American Scholar.*

Sherman Alexie: "Valediction" appeared in *Cave Wall.* Reprinted by permission of the poet.

Rae Armantrout: "Soft Money" from *Money Shot* © 2011 by Rae Armantrout. Reprinted by permission of Wesleyan University Press. Also appeared in *Poetry.*

John Ashbery: "Postlude and Prequel" appeared in *London Review of Books.* Reprinted by permission of the poet.

Julianna Baggott: "To My Lover, Concerning the Yird-Swine" appeared in *AGNI.* Reprinted by permission of the poet.

Erin Belieu: "When at a Certain Party in NYC" appeared in *32 Poems.* Reprinted by permission of the poet.

Cara Benson: "Banking" appeared in *Boston Review.* Reprinted by permission of the poet.

Jaswinder Bolina: "Mine Is the First Rodeo, Mine Is the Last Accolade" appeared in *Black Warrior Review.* Reprinted by permission of the poet.

Catherine Bowman: "The Sink" appeared in *The New Yorker.* Reprinted by permission of the poet.

Turner Cassity: "Off the Nollendorfplatz" appeared in *The Sewanee Review*. Reprinted by permission of The Estate of Turner Cassity.

Michael Cirelli: "Dead Ass" from *Lobster with Ol' Dirty Bastard*. © 2008 by Michael Cirelli. Reprinted by permission of Hanging Loose Press. Also appeared in *The New York Quarterly*.

Billy Collins: "Here and There" appeared in *Boulevard*. Reprinted by permission of the poet.

Olena Kalytiak Davis: "Three Sonnets" appeared in *Green Mountains Review*. Reprinted by permission of the poet.

Matthew Dickman: "Coffee" appeared in *The American Poetry Review*. Reprinted by permission of the poet.

Michael Dickman: "From the Lives of My Friends" from *Flies*. © 2011 by Michael Dickman. Reprinted by permission of Copper Canyon Press. Also appeared in *The New Yorker*.

Denise Duhamel: "My Strip Club" appeared in *DMQ Review*. Reprinted by permission of the poet.

Cornelius Eady: "Emmett Till's Glass-Top Casket" appeared in *The New Yorker*. Reprinted by permission of the poet.

Jill Alexander Essbaum: "Stays" appeared in *Gulf Coast*. Reprinted by permission of the poet.

Alan Feldman: "In November" appeared in *upstreet*. Reprinted by permission of the poet.

Farrah Field: selections from "The Amy Poems" appeared in *LIT*. Reprinted by permission of the poet.

Carolyn Forché: "Morning on the Island" appeared in *The Nation*. Reprinted by permission of the poet.

Beckian Fritz Goldberg: "Everything Is Nervous" appeared in *Michigan Quarterly Review*. Reprinted by permission of the poet.

Benjamin S. Grossberg: "The Space Traveler Talks Frankly about Desire" appeared in *Cave Wall*. Reprinted by permission of the poet.

Jennifer Grotz: "Poppies" appeared in *New England Review*. Reprinted by permission of the poet.

Robert Hass: "August Notebook: A Death" from *The Apple Trees at Olema*. © 2010 by Robert Hass. Reprinted by permission of Ecco/HarperCollins. Also appeared in *The Paris Review*.

Terrance Hayes: "Lighthead's Guide to the Galaxy" from *Lighthead*. © 2010 by Terrance Hayes. Reprinted by permission of Penguin USA. Also appeared in *jubilat*.

K. A. Hays: "Just As, After a Point, Job Cried Out" appeared in *Black Warrior Review*. Reprinted by permission of the poet.